The Germans in the Making of America

by

Frederick Franklin Schrader

1924

THE STRATFORD CO., *Publishers*
BOSTON, MASSACHUSETTS

How many of these same descendants know that to this people belong, by ancestry more or less remote, some of the first scientific men of America, such as the Mühlenbergs, Melsheimer, the "father of American entomology"; Leidy and Gross, the great surgeon; Herkimer, the hero of Oriskany; "Molly Pitcher," the heroine of Monmouth; Post, the Indian missionary, to whom Parkman himself pays a noble tribute; Heckewalder, the Moravian lexicographer of the speech of the Delawares; Armistead, the defender of Fort McHenry in the war of 1812, whose flag, "still there," inspired the Star Spangled Banner; Barbara Frietchie, and General Custer? Surely, this people merit that some slight account be drawn from the mostly unknown books and documents where they have for years reposed, known only to the antiquarians and often veiled from English readers by the German language, in which many of the best and most valuable are written, and given to the English-speaking world of America.—LUCY FORNEY BITTINGER, *The Germans in Colonial Times.* 1901.

CONTENTS

CONTENTS

CONTENTS

CHAPTER X

.

.

THE RACIAL CONTRIBUTIONS TO THE UNITED STATES

By Edw. F. McSweeney, LL. D.

In a general way, the Racial Contribution Series in the Knights of Columbus historical program is intended as a much needed and important contribution to national solidarity. The various studies are treated by able writers, citizens of the United States, each being in full sympathy with the achievements in this country of the racial group of whom he treats. The standard of the writers is the only one that will justify historical writing; — the truth. No censorship has been exercised.

No subject now actively before the people of the United States has been more written on, and less understood, than alien immigration. Until 1819, there were no official statistics of immigration of any sort; the so-called census of 1790 was simply a report of the several states of their male white population under and over 16 years of age, all white females, slaves, and others. Statements as to the country of origin of the inhabitants of this country were, in the main, guesswork, with the result that, while the great bulk of such estimates was honestly and patriotically done, some of the most quoted during the present day were inspired, obviously to prove a predetermined case, rather than to recite the ascertained fact.

From the beginning the dominant groups in control in the United States have regarded each group of newer arrivals as more or less the "enemy" to be feared, and, if possible, controlled. A study of various cross-sections of the country will show dominant alien groups who formerly had to fight for their very existence. With increased numerical strength and prosperity they frequently attempted to do to the later aliens, frequently even of their own group, what had formerly been done to them: — decry and stifle their achievements, and deny them opportunity, — the one thing that may justly be demanded in a Democracy, — by putting them in a position of inferiority.

To attempt, in this country, to set up a "caste" control, based on the accident of birth, wealth, or privilege, is a travesty of Democracy. When Washington and his compatriots, a group comprising the most efficiently prepared men in the history of the world, who had set themselves definitely to form a democratic civilization, dreamed of and even planned by Plato, but held back by slavery and paganism, they found their sure foundations in the precepts of Christianity, and gave them expression in the Declaration of Independence. The liberty they sought, based on obedience to the law of God as well as of man, was actually established, but from the beginning it has met a constant effort to substitute some form of absolutism tending to break down or replace democratic institutions.

What may be called, for want of a better term, the colonial spirit, which is the essence of hyphenism, has persisted in this country to hamper national progress and national unity. Wherever this colonial spirit shows itself it is a menace to be fought, whether the secret or acknowledged attachment binds to England, Ireland, France, Germany, Italy, Greece or any other nation.

Jefferson pointed out that we have on this soil evolv·s a new race of men who may inexactly be called "Americans". This term, as a monopoly of the United States, is properly objected to by our neighbors, North and South — yet it has a definite meaning for the world.

During the Great War one aspect of war duty was to direct the labor activities growing out of the war, to divert labor from "non-essential" to "essential" industry and to arbitrate and mediate on wage matters. It was found necessary to study and to analyze the greatly feared, but infrequently discovered "enemy alien"; and as a preparation for this duty, with the assistance of several hundred local agents, the population of Massachusetts was separated into naturally allied groups based on birth, racial descent, religious, social and industrial affiliations. The astonishing result was that, counting as "native Americans" only the actual descendants of all those living in Massachusetts in 1840, of whatever racial stock prior to that time, only two-sevenths, even with the most liberal classification, came within the group of colonial descent, while the remaining five-sevenths were found in the various racial groups coming later than 1840. More than this: While the "Colonial" group had increased in numbers for three decades after 1840, in 1918 they were found actually to be fewer in number than in 1840, a diminution due to excess of deaths over births, proceeding in increasing ratio.

Membership in the Society of Mayflower descendants is eagerly sought as the hallmark of American ancestry. In anticipation of the tercentenary of the Mayflower-coming in 1620, about a dozen years ago a questionnaire was sent to every known eligible for Mayflower ancestry, and the replies were submitted to the experts in one of the national universities for review and report. When this report was presented later, it contained the statement that, considering the prevailing number of marriages in this group, and children per family, — when the six-hundredth celebration of the Pilgrims' Landing is held in 2220, three hundred years hence, a ship the size of the original Mayflower will be sufficient to carry back to Europe all the then living Mayflower descendants.

The future of America is in the keeping of the 80 per cent. of the population, separate in blood and race from the colonial descent group. Love of native land is one of the strongest and noblest passions of which a man is capable. Family life, religion, the soil which holds the dust of our fathers, sentiment for ancestral property, and many other bonds, make the ties of home so strong and enduring, and unite a man's life so closely with its native environment, that grave and powerful reasons must exist before a change of residence is contemplated. Escape from religious persecution and political tyranny were unquestionably the chief reasons which induced the early comers to America to brave the dangers of an unknown world. Yet that very intolerance against which this was a protest soon began to be exercised against all those unwilling to accept in their new homes the religious leadership of those in control.

It is not necessary to go into the persecutions due to religious bigotry of the colonial period. While the spirit of liberty was in the free air of the colonies and would finally have secured national independence, it is not possible to underestimate the support brought to the revolting colonials because of the attitude of Great Britain in allowing religious freedom to Canada after it had been taken from the French. After the victory of New Orleans, a spirit of national consciousness on a democratic basis was built up and the narrow spirit of colonialism and of religious intolerance was to a great degree repudiated by the people, when they had become inspired with the American spirit, — only to be revived later on.

The continued manifestation of intolerance has been the most persistent effort in our national life. It has done incalculable harm. It is apparently deep-rooted, an active force in almost every generation. Present in the 30's, 40's and 50's, stopped temporarily for two decades by the Civil War, it has recurred subsequently again and again; revived since the Armistice, it is unfortunately shown to-day in as great a virulence and power of destructiveness as at any time during the last hundred years.

After the 70's, as the aliens became numerically powerful and began to demand political representation, movements based on religious prejudice were started from time to time, some of which came to temporary prominence, later to die an inglorious death; but all these movements which attempted to deprive aliens of their right of freedom to worship were calculated to bring economic discontent and to add to the measure of national disunion and unhappiness.

Sixty years ago[1] the bigoted slogan was *"No Irish need apply."* During the World War, the principal attack was on the German-American citizens of this country, whose fathers had come here seeking a new land as a protest against tyranny. To-day the current attempt is

---

[1] In the fifties it was customary for the merchants, etc., to have posted at their door a list of help wanted. Many of these help wanted signs were accompanied by another which read "No Irish need apply." During the Civil War there was an Anti-Draft song with a refrain to the effect that when it came to drafting they did not practice "No Irish need apply."

to deprive the Jews[2] of the right to educational equality. In short, while there have been spasmodic manifestations of movements based on intolerance in many countries, the United States has the unenviable record for continuous effort to keep alive a bogey based on an increasing fear of something which never existed, and cannot ever exist in this country.

For a hundred years the potent cause which has poured millions of human beings into the United States has been its marvellous opportunities, and unprecedented economic urge. Ever since 1830 a graphic chart of the variations in immigration from year to year will reflect the industrial situation in the United States for the same period. In 1837, the total immigration was 79,430.[3] After the panic of that year it decreased in 1838 to 38,914.[4] In 1842, it increased to 104,565,[5] but a business depression in 1844 caused it to shrink to 78,615.[6] Thus the influx of aliens increased or decreased according to the industrial conditions prevalent here. The business prosperity of the United States was not only the urge to entice immigrants hither, but it made their coming possible as they were helped by the savings of relatives and friends already here.

The English were not immigrants, but colonists, merely going from one part of national territory to another. With few exceptions, the majority of the early colonists came from England. The first English settlement was made in Virginia under the London Company

---

[2] "Americans only" in a real estate advertisement to-day usually means "No Jews need apply." It sometimes means Irish (i. e., Catholic) also.

[3] Wm. J. Bromwell, *History of Immigration to United States*, p. 96.

[4] *Ibid.*, p. 100.

[5] *Ibid.*, p. 116.

[6] *Ibid.*, p. 124.

in 1607. It took twelve years of hard struggling to establish this colony on a permanent basis.

The New England region was settled by a different class of colonists. Plymouth was the first settlement, in 1620, followed in 1630 by the Massachusetts Bay Colony, which later absorbed the Plymouth settlement. Population, after the first ten years, increased rapidly by natural growth, and soon colonies in Rhode Island, New Hampshire and Connecticut resulted from the overflow in the original settlements.

While this English settlement was going on North and South, the Dutch, under the Dutch West India Company, took possession of the region between, and founded New Netherlands and New Amsterdam, later New York City. Intervening, as it did, between their Northern and Southern colonies, New Netherlands, which the English considered a menace, was seized by the English during a war with Holland, and became New York and New Jersey.

Early in the seventeenth century there was a substantial French immigration to the Dutch colonies. There was a constant stream of French immigration to the English colonies in New England and in Virginia by many of the Huguenots who had originally emigrated to the West Indies.

In 1681, Penn settled Pennsylvania under a royal charter and thus the whole Atlantic coast from Canada to Florida became subject to England. During the colonial period, England contributed to the population of the colonies. But, by the middle of the seventeenth century, the coming of the English to New England was practically over. From 1628 to 1641 about 20,000 came from England to New England, but for the next century and a half more persons went back to Old England than came from there to New England.[7] Due to the relaxing of religious persecution of dissenting Protestants in England, the great formerly impelling force to seek a new home across the ocean in America had ceased.

In 1653 an Irish immigration to New England, much larger in numbers than the original Plymouth Colony, was proposed. Bristol merchants, who realized the necessity of populating the colonies to make them prosperous, treated with the government for men, women and girls to be sent to the West Indies and to New England.[8] At the very fountain head of American life we find, therefore, men and women of pure Celtic blood from the South of Ireland, infused into the primal stock of America. But these apparently were only a drop in this early tide of Irish immigration.[9]

[7] *Commercial Relations of the United States,* 1885-1886, Appendix III, p. 1967.

[8] "The Commissioners for Ireland gave them orders upon the governors of garrisons, to deliver to them prisoners of war; upon the keepers of gaols, for offenders in custody; upon masters of workhouses, for the destitute in their care 'who were of an age to labor, or if women were marriageable and not past breeding'; and gave directions to all in authority to seize those who had no visible means of livelihood, and deliver them to these agents of the Bristol sugar merchants, in execution of which latter direction Ireland must have exhibited scenes in every part like the slave hunts in Africa. How many girls of gentle birth have been caught and hurried to the private prisons of these man-catchers none can tell. Messrs. Sellick and Leader, Mr. Robert Yeomans, Mr. Joseph Lawrence, and others, all of Bristol, were active agents. As one instance out of many: Captain John Vernon was employed by the Commissioners for Ireland into England, and contracted in their behalf with Mr. David Sellick and Mr. Leader under his hand, bearing date the 14th September, 1653, to supply them with two hundred and fifty women of the Irish nation above twelve years, and under the age of forty-five, also three hundred men above twelve years of age, and under fifty, to be found in the country within twenty miles of Cork, Youghal, and Kinsale, Waterford and Wexford, to transport them into New England." J. P. Prendergast, *The Cromwellian Settlement of Ireland,* London, 1865. 2d. ed., pp. 89-90.

[9] "It is calculated that in four years (1653-1657) English firms of slave-dealers shipped 6,400 Irish men and women, boys and maidens, to the British colonies of North America." A. J. Theband, *The Irish Race in the Past and Present,* N. Y., 1893, p. 385.

No complete memorial has been transmitted of the emigrations that took place from Europe to America, but (from the few illustrative facts actually preserved) they seem to have been amazingly copious. In the years 1771-72, the number of emigrants to America from the North of Ireland alone amounted to 17,350. Almost all of these emigrated at their own charge; a great majority of them were persons employed in the linen manufacture, or farmers possessed of some property which they converted into money and carried with them. Within the first fortnight of August, 1773, there arrived at Philadelphia 3,500 emigrants from Ireland, and from the same document which has recorded this circumstance it appears that vessels were arriving every month freighted with emigrants from Holland, Germany, and especially from Ireland and the Highlands of Scotland.[10]

That many Irish settled in Maryland is shown by the fact that in 1699 and again a few years later an act was passed to prevent too great a number of Irish Papists being imported into the province.[11] Shipmasters were required to pay two shillings per poll for such. "Shipping records of the colonial period show that boatload after boatload left the southern and eastern shores of Ireland for the New World. Undoubtedly thousands of their passengers were Irish of the native stock."[12] So besides the so-called Scotch-Irish from the North of Ireland, the distinction always being Protestantism, not race, it is indisputable that thousands, Celtic in race and Catholic in religion, came to the colonies. These newcomers made

[10] Rev. T. A. Spencer, *History of the United States*, Vol. 1, p. 305.
[11] Henry Pratt Fairchild, *Immigration: A world movement, and its American significance*, N. Y., 1913, p. 47. See also *Archives of Maryland*, Vol. 22, p. 497.
[12] Charles A. and Mary R. Beard, *History of the United States*, N. Y., 1921, p. 11.

their homes principally in Pennsylvania, Virginia, Maryland, the Carolinas and the frontiers of the New England colonies. Later they pushed on westward and founded Ohio, Kentucky and Tennessee. An interesting essay by the well-known writer, Irvin S. Cobb, on *The Lost Irish Tribes in the South* is an important contribution to this subject.

The Germans were the next most important element of the early population of America. A number of the artisans and carpenters in the first Jamestown colony were of German descent. In 1710, a body of 3,000 Germans came to New York — the largest number of immigrants supposed to have arrived at one time during the colonial period.[18] Most of the early German immigrants settled in New Jersey, the Carolinas, and Pennsylvania. It has been estimated that at the end of the colonial period the number of Germans was fully two hundred thousand.

Though the Irish and the Germans contributed most largely to colonial immigration, as distinguished from the English, who are classed as the Colonials, there were other races who came even thus early to our shores. The Huguenots came from France to escape religious persecution. The Jews, then as ever, engaged in their age-old struggle for religious and economic toleration, came from England, France, Spain and Portugal. The Dutch Government of New Amsterdam, fearing their commercial competition, ordered a group of Portuguese Jews to leave the colony, but this decision was appealed to the home Government at Holland and reversed, so that they were allowed to remain. On the whole, their freedom to live and to trade in the colonies was so much greater than in their former homes that there were soon flourishing

[18] Fairchild, p. 35.

colonies of Jewish merchants in Newport, Philadelphia and Charleston.

In 1626 a company of Swedish merchants organized, under the patronage of the Great King Gustavus Adolphus, to promote immigration to America. The King contributed four hundred thousand dollars to the capital raised, but did not live to see the fruition of his plans. In 1637, the first company of Swedes and Finns left Stockholm for America. They reached Delaware Bay and called the country New Sweden. The Dutch claimed, by right of priority, this same territory and in 1655 the flag of Holland replaced that of Sweden. The small Swedish colony in Delaware came under Penn's rule and became, like Pennsylvania, cosmopolitan in character.

The Dutch in New York preserved their racial characteristics for more than a hundred years after the English conquest of 1664. At the end of the colonial period, over one-half of the 170,000 inhabitants of New York were descendants of the original Dutch.

Many of the immigrants who came here in the early days paid their own passage. However, the actual number of such is only a matter of conjecture. From the shipping records of the period we do know positively that thousands came who were unable to pay. Shipowners and others who had the means furnished the passage money to those too poor to pay for themselves, and in return received from these persons a promise or bond. This bond provided that the person named in it should work for a certain number of years to repay the money advanced. Such persons were called "indentured servants" and they were found throughout the colonies, working in the fields, the shops and the homes of the colonists. The term of service was from five to seven years. Many found it impossible to meet their obligations and their servitude dragged on for years. Others, on the contrary, became free and prosperous. In Pennsylvania often there were as many as fifty bond servants on estates. The condition of indentured servants in Virginia "was little better than that of slaves. Loose indentures and harsh laws put them at the mercy of their masters."[14] This seems to have been their fate in all the colonies, as their treatment depended upon the character of their masters.

Besides these indentured servants who came here voluntarily, a large number of early settlers were forced to come here. The Irish before mentioned are one example. In order to secure settlers, men, women and children were kidnapped from the cities and towns and "spirited away" to America by the companies and proprietors who had colonies here. In 1680 it was officially computed that 10,000 were sent thus to American shores. In 1627, about 1,500 children were shipped to Virginia, probably orphans and dependents whom their relatives were unwilling to support.[15] Another class sent here were convicts, the scourings of English centers like Bristol and Liverpool. The colonists protested vehemently against this practise, but it was continued up to the very end of the colonial period, when this convict tide was diverted to "Botany Bay."

In 1619, another race was brought here against their will and sold into slavery. This was the Negro, forced to leave his home near the African equator that he might contribute to the material wealth of shipmasters and planters. Slowly but surely chattel slavery took firm root in the South and at last became the leading source of the

[14] Henry Cabot Lodge, *A Short History of the English Colonies in America*, N. Y., 1881, p. 70.
[15] Beard, p. 15.

labor supply. The slave traders found it very easy to seize Negroes in Africa and make great profits by selling them in Southern ports. The English Royal African Company sent to America annually between 1713 and 1743 from 5,000 to 10,000 slaves.[16] After a time, when the Negroes were so numerous that whole sections were overrun, the Southern colonies tried ineffectually to curb the trade. Virginia in 1710 placed a duty of five pounds on each slave but the Royal Governor vetoed the bill. Bills of like import were passed in other colonies from time to time, but the English crown disapproved in every instance and the trade, so lucrative to British shipowners, went on. At the time of the Revolution, there were almost half a million slaves in the colonies.[17] The exact proportions of the slave trade to America can be but approximately determined. From 1680 to 1688 the African Company sent 249 ships to Africa, shipped there 60,783 Negro slaves, and after losing 14,387 on the middle passage, delivered 46,396 in America. The trade increased early in the eighteenth century, 104 ships clearing for Africa in 1701; it then dwindled until the signing of the Assiento, standing at 74 clearances in 1724. The final dissolution of the monopoly in 1750 led — excepting in the years 1754-57, when the closing of Spanish marts sensibly affected the trade — to an extraordinary development, 192 clearances being made in 1771. The Revolutionary War nearly stopped the traffic, but by 1786 the clearances had risen again to 146.

To these figures must be added the unregistered trade of Americans and foreigners. It is probable that about 25,000 slaves were brought to America each year between

[16] Beard, p. 16.
[17] W. S. Burghardt DuBois, *Suppression of the Slave Trade,* Harvard Historical Studies, No. 1, p. 5.

1698 and 1707. The importation then dwindled but after the Assiento rose to perhaps 30,000. The proportion of these slaves carried to the continent now began to increase. Of about 20,000 whom the English annually imported from 1733 to 1766, South Carolina alone received some 3,000. Before the Revolution the total exportation to America is variously estimated as between 40,000 and 100,000 each year. Bancroft places the total slave population of the continental colonies at 59,000 in 1714; 78,000 in 1727; and 293,000 in 1754. The census of 1790 showed 697,897 slaves in the United States. Not all the Negroes who came to America were slaves and not all remained slaves. There were the following free Negroes in the decades between 1790 and 1860:

1790	59,557
1800	108,435
1810	186,446
1820	233,634
1830	319,599
1840	386,293
1850	434,495
1860	488,070

Immigration of Negroes is still taking place, especially from the West Indies. It has been estimated that there are the following foreign-born Negroes in the United States:

1890	19,979
1900	20,336
1910	40,339
1920	75,000

In 1790, Negroes were one-fifth of the total population; in 1860 they were one-seventh; in 1900 one-ninth;[12] to-day they are approximately one-tenth.

With the beginning of the national era — 1783 — all peoples subsequently coming to the United States must be classed as immigrants. During the first years of our national life, no accurate statistics of immigration were kept. The Federal Government took no control of the matter and the State records are incomplete and unreliable. A pamphlet published by the Bureau of Statistics in 1903, *Immigration into the United States,* says, "The best estimates of the total immigration into the United States prior to the official count puts the total number of arrivals at not to exceed 250,000 in the entire period between 1776 and 1820."

From 1806 to 1816, the unfriendly relations which existed between the United States and England and France precluded any extensive immigration to this country. England maintained and for a time successfully enforced the doctrine that "a man once a subject was always a subject." The American Merchant Service, because of the pay and good treatment given, was very attractive to English sailors and a very great enticement to them to come to America and enter the American service. However, the fear of impressment deterred many from so doing. The Blockade Decrees of England against France in 1806 and the retaliation decrees of France against England in that same year were other influences which retarded immigration. These decrees were succeeded by the British Orders in Council, the Milan Decree of Napoleon, and the United States law of 1809 prohibiting intercourse with both Great Britain and France.

[12] John R. Commons, *Races and Immigrants in America,* N. Y., 1907, p. 53.

In 1810, the French decrees were annulled and American commerce began again with France, only to have the vessels fall into the hands of the British. Then came the War of 1812. The German immigration suffered greatly from this condition of affairs, as the Germans sailed principally from the ports of Liverpool and Havre. At these points ships were more numerous and expenses less heavy. In December, 1814, a few days before the Battle of New Orleans, a treaty of peace was concluded between the United States and England and after a few months immigration was resumed once more.

In 1817, about 22,240 persons arrived at ports of the United States from foreign countries. This number included American citizens returning from abroad. In no previous year had so many immigrants come to our shores.

In 1819 a law was passed by Congress and approved by the President "regulating passenger ships and vessels." In 1820, the official history of immigration began. The Port Collectors then began to keep records which included numbers, sexes, ages, and occupations of all incoming persons. However, up to 1856, no distinction was made between travellers and immigrants.

Immigration increased from 8,358 in 1820 — of which 6,024 came from Great Britain and Ireland — to 22,633 in 1831.[19] The decade of the twenties was a time of great industrial activity in the United States. The Erie Canal was built, other canals were projected, the railroads were started, business increased by leaps and bounds. As a consequence, the demand for labor was imperative and Europe responded. During the entire period of our

---

[19] Adam Seybert, *Statistical Annals of the United States,* Phila., 1818, p. 29.

early national life, the United States encouraged the coming of foreign artisans and laborers as the necessity for strength, skill and courage in the upbuilding of our country began to be realized.

From 1831 the number of immigrants steadily increased until from September 30, 1849, to September 30, 1850, they totaled 315,334[20] The largest increases during those years were from 1845 to 1848, when the famine in Ireland and the revolution in Germany drove thousands to the shores of free America. These causes continued to increase the number of arrivals until in 1854 the crest was attained with 460,474[21] — a figure not again reached for nearly twenty years.

From September 30, 1819, when the official count of immigrants began to be taken, to December 31, 1855, a total of 4,212,624 persons of foreign birth arrived in the United States.[22] Of these Bromwell, who wrote in 1856 a work compiled entirely from official data, estimates that 1,747,930 were Irish.[23] Next comes Germany,[24] with 1,206,087; England third with 207,492; France fourth with 188,725.

The exodus of the Irish during those famine years furnishes one of the many examples recorded in history of a subject race driven from its home by the economic injustice of a dominant race. Later, we see the same thing true in Austria-Hungary where the Slavs were tyrannized by the Magyars; again we find it in Russia where the Jew sought freedom from the Slav; and once again in Armenia and Syria where the native people fled from the Turk.

[20] Young, *Special Report on Immigration*, Phila., 1871, p. 5.
[21] Bromwell, p. 145.
[22] *Ibid.*, p. 16.
[23] *Ibid.*, p. 18.
[24] *Ibid.*, pp. 16-17.

After 1855, the tide of immigration began to decrease steadily. During the first two years of the Civil War, it was less than 100,000.[25] In 1863, an increase was noticeable again and 395,922[26] immigrants are recorded in 1869.

During all these years up to 1870, the great part of the immigration was from Northern Europe. The largest racial groups were composed of Irish, Germans, Scandinavians and French. About the middle of the nineteenth century French-speaking Canadians were attracted by the opportunities for employment in the mills and factories of New England.

The number of Irish coming here steadily decreased after 1880 until it has fallen far below that of other European peoples. Altogether, the total Irish immigration from 1820 to 1906 is placed at something over 4,000,000, thus giving the Irish second place as contributors to the foreign-born population of the United States. The Revolution of 1848 was the contributing cause of a large influx of Germans, many of whom were professional men and artisans. From 1873 to 1879 there was great industrial depression in Germany and consequently another large immigration to America took place. Since 1882, there has also been a noticeable decline in German immigrants. From 1820 to 1903, a total of over 5,000,000 Germans was recorded as coming to the United States.[27]

In the period from 1880 to 1910 immigration from Italy totaled 4,018,404. It will be remembered that the law requiring the registration of outgoing aliens was not passed until 1908, and it may, therefore, be estimated that

[25] Young, p. 6.
[26] Ibid., p. 6.
[27] Special Consular Reports, Vol. 30, p. 8.

3,000,000 represents the total number of arrivals from Italy, who remained here permanently.

After 1903, up to the outbreak of the Great War, the number of alien arrivals steadily increased. In 1905, it was more than 1,000,000; in 1906, it passed the 1,100,000 mark and in 1907 the 1,200,000 mark; in 1913 and 1914, the total number for each year exceeded 1,400,000.[28]

During the ten years from 1905 to 1915, nearly 12,-000,000 aliens landed in the United States, a yearly average of 1,200,000 arrivals. These alone form more than 37 per cent. of all recorded immigration since 1820 and make up about 88 out of every 100 of our present total foreign-born population.[29]. Until interrupted by the European War, the immigration to the United States was the greatest movement of the largest number of peoples that the world has ever known. Of course, there have been economic upheavals from time to time which have noticeably affected this movement. The Civil War, as before noted, and financial panics and industrial depressions in our country interrupted the incoming tide repeatedly. The Great War with its social and economic upheaval had a tremendous effect on our immigration. The twelve months following the declaration of war shows the smallest number of alien arrivals since 1899. The number was slightly over 325,000. The statistics compiled by the Federal Bureau of Immigration show that by far the greater part of the immigrants who come to the United States are from Europe. Of the 1,403,00 alien immigrants who came here in 1914, about 1,114,00 were from Europe; about 35,000 came from Asia; the remainder, about 254,000, came from all other countrie

[28] *Immigration and Emigration*, Bureau of Labor Statistics, Washington, 1915, p. 1099.
[29] *Ibid.*

combined, principally Canada, the West Indies, and Mexico. Eighty out of every 100, therefore, came from Europe. As many as sixty of that eighty came from the three countries of Italy, Austria-Hungary and Russia. Italy sent 294,689; Austria-Hungary was second with 286,059; Russian contributed 262,409. From all of England, Ireland, Scotland and Wales came only 88,000 or about 6 out of every 100; and from Norway, Sweden and Denmark came about 31,000 or 2 out of every 100.

Greece, France, Portugal, Bulgaria, Montenegro, Spain, Turkey, the Netherlands, Belgium, Switzerland, and Roumania contributed virtually all the remainder of our 1914 immigrants from Europe, given in the order of importance.

However, we should bear in mind always that the country of origin or nationality or jurisdiction (as determined by political boundaries) is not always identical with race. Immigration statistics have followed national or political boundaries. Take the immigrants from Russia. The statistics say that 262,000 arrived from that country in 1914. But of this number, less than 5 out of every 100 are Russians; the rest or 95 out of every 100, are Hebrews, Poles, Lithuanians, Finns and Germans.

Austria-Hungary was another country made of a medley of races. The Germanic Austrians who ruled Austria and the Hungarian Magyars who ruled Hungary were less than one-half of the total population of the one time Austria-Hungary.

The record of alien arrivals from Poland is not accurate because it is divided into three national statistical divisions — Russia, Germany and Austria-Hungary. The best estimate is that the total Polish arrivals to the United States since 1820 approximates 2,500,000.

The Slav, the Magyar, the German, the Latin, and the Jew were all in Austria-Hungary and moreover, these were all numerously subdivided. The most numerous of the Slavs are the Czechs and Slovaks. These gave the United States in 1914 a combined immigration of 37,000. Poles, Ruthenians and Roumanians also came here from northern Austria, and from the vicinity of the Black Sea came Roumanians more Latin than Slavic. Besides these, the one time dual kingdom sent Jews, Greeks and Turks.

Although the most important Slavic country of Europe is Russia, yet it was from Austria-Hungary that we received most of our Slavic immigrants. In 1914, as many as 23 out of every 100 of our total immigration were Slavic, and the larger part of this racial group which reached 319,000 that year, came from Austria-Hungary.

That mere recording of country or origin does not give accurate racial information is illustrated in the case of the many Greeks under Turkish rule, and the large number of Armenians found in almost all large Turkish towns. The Armenians are probably the most numerous of the immigrants from Asia. In 1914, the total immigration from Turkey was about 20,000, but the actual Turkish immigration was only 3,000. The remaining 27,000 were Greeks, Bulgarians, Serbians, Montenegrins, Syrians, Armenians and Hebrews.[20]

The "country of origin" tells us almost nothing about the large Hebrew immigration which comes to the United States. The Jew comes from many countries. The greater part of all our recent Jewish immigration comes from Russia, from what is called the "Jewish Pale of Settlement" in the western part of that country. Other Jews come from Austria, Roumania, Germany and Tur-

[20] *Reports of Department of Labor,* Washington, 1915.

key. In 1914, the Jews were the fourth largest in numbers among our immigrants, nearly 143,000.[21]

We must also bear in mind that all of these millions who came to America do not remain with us. There is a constant emigration going on, a departure of aliens back to their native land either for a time, or for all time. Up to 1908, the Bureau of Immigration kept no record of the "ebb of the tide" but since that time vessels taking aliens out of the United States, are obliged by law to make a list containing name, age, sex, nationality, residence in the United States, occupation, and time of last arrival of each alien passenger, which must be filed with the Federal Collector of Customs.

The first year of this record, 1908, followed the financial panic of October, 1907, and due to the economic conditions prevalent in the United States a very large emigration to Europe was disclosed.

The records show also that the volume of emigration, like that of immigration, varies from year to year. Just as prosperity here increases immigration, "bad" times increase emigration from our shores.

There was a time when emigration was so slight that it was of little importance, but since the early nineties it has assumed large proportions. After the panic of 1907, for months a larger number left the country than came into it, and thousands and thousands swarmed the ports of departure awaiting a chance to return home. In the earlier years, the immigrant sometimes spent months making the journey here. Besides the difficulty of the trip, ocean transportation was more expensive. Therefore, the earlier immigrants came to remain, to make homes here for themselves and their children. The Irish, the Ger-

[21] *Ibid.*

mans, the early Bohemians, the Scandinavians, and in fact all the early comers brought their families and their "household goods", ready to settle down for all time and to become citizens of their adopted country.

A large number of the alien arrivals of recent years come here initially with only a vague intention of remaining permanently, and these make up the large emigration streaming constantly from our ports. However, it is only fair to say that eventually many of these people come back to America and become permanent residents. Anyone who has had experience at our ports of entry can substantiate the statement that during a period of years the same faces are seen incoming again and again.

Although immigrants have come by millions into the United States, and have been the main contributing cause of its wonderful national expansion, yet opposition to their coming has manifested itself strongly at different times.

In the colonial period the people objected, and rightly to the maternal solicitude which England evidenced by making the colonies the dumping ground for criminal and undesirables. However, these objections were disregarded and convicts and criminals continued to come while the colonies remained under British rule.

After the national era, immigration was practically unrestricted down to 1875. At different periods there were manifestations of a strong desire to restrict immigration, but Congress never responded with exclusion laws. The alien and sedition laws of 1798 had for their object the removal of foreigners already residents in the United States. The naturalization laws passed that same year lengthening the time of residence necessary for citizenship to fourteen years, were another severe measure against resident aliens. The native American and the Know-nothing uprisings were still other indications of that same spirit of antagonism to the alien based on religious grounds. This religious antagonism in many of the States took the form of opposition to immigration itself and a demand for restrictions. But this all proved futile, for the National Government recognized the necessity of settling the limitless West. Then, too, another subject loomed large and threatening at this time, and engrossed the attention of the people away from the dire evils which the Irish and the Catholics would precipitate upon "our free and happy people". This was the State Rights and Slavery question; and soon the country forgot immigration in the throes of the Civil War.

By an act of March 3, 1875, the National Government made its first attempt to restrict immigration; this act prohibited the bringing in of alien convicts and of women for immoral purposes. On May 6, 1882, Congress passed and the President approved another act "to regulate immigration", by which the coming of Chinese laborers was forbidden for ten years. The story which led up to this Act of Congress is a long one, and the details cannot be given here. Briefly, conditions in California following the Burlingame treaty of 1868, owning to the influx of Chinese labor, resulted in the organization of a working-man's party headed by Dennis Kearney, and forced the Chinese question as one of the dominant issues of State politics. Resolutions embodying the feelings of the people on Chinese immigration were presented to the Constitutional Convention of 1879. The State Legislature enacted laws against this immigration. Subsequently pressure was brought to bear on the National Government, a new treaty with China was negotiated, and finally the law of 1882 was passed by Congress, restricting for ten years the admission of Chinese laborers, both skilled and unskilled, and of mine workers also.

Ever since the passage of this law, the Federal Government has pursued a more restrictive and exclusive immigration policy. The next law was passed in August, 1882, prohibiting the immigration of "any convict, lunatic, idiot, or any person unable to take care of himself or herself without becoming a public charge." Then, in 1885, came another act known as the "Alien Contract Labor Law", forbidding the importation and immigration of foreigners and aliens under contract or agreement to perform labor in the United States. In 1891 came the law called the "Geary Act" which amended "the various acts relative to immigration and the importation of aliens under contract or agreement to perform labor". This act extended Chinese exclusion for another ten years, and required the Chinese in the country to register and submit to the Bertillon test as a means of identification. In 1893 two acts were passed; one which gave the quarantine service greater powers and placed additional duties upon the Public Health Service, and another which properly enforced the existing immigration and contract labor laws. In 1902 the law of exclusion was made permanent against Chinese laborers. So, since 1875, the United States has passed laws excluding Chinese entirely and virtually excluding the Japanese, and both these races are ineligible to citizenship. In 1907, an act was passed "to regulate the immigration of Aliens into the United States", which excluded imbeciles, epileptics, those so defective either physically or mentally that they might become public charges; children under sixteen not with a parent, etc.

A far more restrictive measure known as the "literacy"

or "educational" test has been before Congress at different times and has, on three different occasions, falied to become a law. President Cleveland vetoed it in 1897, Taft in 1913, and Wilson in 1915. All three Presidents objected to this bill principally on the ground that it was such "a radical departure" from all previous national policy in regard to immigration. President Wilson's veto of 1917 was overcome and the bill became a law by a two-thirds majority vote of both houses. This law requires that entering aliens must be able to read the English language or some other language or dialect. The one thing which the literacy test was designed to accomplish — to decrease the volume of immigration — was brought about suddenly and unexpectedly by the European War. From the opening of the war, the number of immigrants steadily decreased until, for the year ending June 30, 1916, it was only 298,826[32] and for the year ending June 30, 1917, only 110,618.[33] Then it began again to increase steadily until for the year ending June 30, 1920, it reached a total of 430,001.[34]

On June 3, 1921, an emergency measure known as the three per cent. law was passed. This act provided that the number of aliens of any nationality who could be admitted to the United States in any one year should be limited to three per cent. of the number of foreign-born persons of such nationality resident in the United States as determined by the census of 1910. Certain ones were not counted, such as foreign government officials and their families and employees, aliens in transit through the United States, tourists, aliens from countries having immigration treaties with the United States, aliens who

[32] *Reports of Department of Labor,* Washington, 1918, p. 208.
[33] *Reports of Department of Labor,* Washington, 1920, p. 400.
[34] *Reports of Department of Labor,* Washington, 1921, p. 365.

have lived for one year previous to their admission in Canada, Newfoundland, Mexico, Central America, or South America, and aliens under eighteen who have parents who are American citizens. More than twenty per cent. of a country's full quota could not be admitted in one month except in the case of actors, artists, lecturers, singers, nurses, clergymen, professors, members of the learned professions or domestic servants who could always come in even though the month's or the year's quota had been used.

A well organized effort is under way in the Congress which began its session in December 1923, to reduce the quota to two per cent. of the immigrants recorded as coming to the United States in 1890. This bill, which will probably be passed, is being opposed vigorously, by the Jews and Italians who are immediately the particular racial groups to be affected, but since neither the Jews nor Italians, separately or collectively, have political strength to be a voting factor to be considered, except in a half dozen of the industrial states, the passage of the bill seems to be inevitable.

The recent immigration restriction laws make a decided break with past national history and tradition. There is little doubt that these laws are in part the fruit of an organized movement which, especially since the war, is attempting to classify all aliens, except those of one special group, as "hyphenates" and "mongrels". These laws are haphazard, unscientific, based on unworthy prejudice and likely, ultimately, to be disastrous in their economic consequences. The present three per cent. immigration law is not based on any fundamental standard of fitness. Once the percentage of maximum admissions is reached, in any given month, the next alien applying for

entrance may be a potential Washington, Lincoln or
Edison to whom the unyielding process of the law must
deny admission.   Such laws, worked out under the hysteria
of "after war psychology", seem to be one of the instances,
so frequent in history, where Democracy must take time
to work out its own mistakes.

Under the circumstances, there is all the more reason
that the priceless heritage of racial achievement by the
descendants of various racial groups in the United States
be told.

The United States has departed a long way from the
policy which was recorded in 1795 by the series of coins
known as the "Liberty and Security" coins, on which
appeared the words "A Refuge for the Oppressed of all
Nations".

ARRIVALS OF ALIEN PASSENGERS AND IMMIGRANTS IN THE UNITED STATES FROM 1820 TO 1892

Prepared by the Bureau of Statistics and published in 1898 by the Government Printing Office.

Countries Whence Arrived	1821 to 1830	1831 to 1840	1841 to 1850	1851 to Dec. 31, 1860	Jan. 1 1861 to June 30, 1870	Fiscal Years 1871 to 1880	Fiscal Years 1881 to 1890	Fiscal Years 1891 and 1892	Total
Austria-Hungary	27	22	...	...	7,800	72,969	353,719	151,178	595,666
Belgium	169	1,063	5,074	4,738	6,734	7,221	20,177	7,340	51,533
Denmark	...	639	539	3,749	17,094	31,771	88,132	21,282	163,769
France	8,497	45,575	77,262	76,358	35,984	72,206	50,464	13,291	879,637
Germany	6,761	152,454	434,626	951,667	787,468	718,182	1,452,970	244,312	4,743,440
Italy	408	2,253	1,870	9,231	11,728	55,759	307,309	138,191	526,749
Netherlands	1,078	1,412	8,251	10,789	9,102	16,541	53,701	12,466	113,340
Norway and Sweden	91	1,201	13,903	20,931	109,298	211,245	568,362	107,167	1,032,188
Russia and Poland	91	646	656	1,621	4,536	52,254	265,088	192,615	617,507
Spain and Portugal	2,622	2,954	2,759	10,353	8,493	9,393	6,535	5,657	49,266
Switzerland	3,226	4,821	4,644	25,011	23,286	28,293	81,988	14,219	185,488
United Kingdom.									
England (a)	22,167	73,143	263,332	385,643	568,128	460,479	657,488	104,675	2,534,955
Scotland	2,912	2,667	3,712	38,331	38,769	87,564	149,869	24,077	347,900
Ireland	50,724	207,381	780,719	914,119	435,778	436,871	655,482	111,173	3,592,247
Total United Kingdom	75,803	283,191	1,047,763	1,338,093	1,042,674	984,914	1,462,839	289,925	6,476,102
All other countries of Europe.	43	96	165	116	210	656	10,318	4,964	16,543
Total Europe.	98,816	495,688	1,697,502	2,452,657	2,064,407	2,261,904	4,721,602	b1,152,487	14,846,063
British North American Possessions.	2,277	13,624	41,723	59,309	153,871	383,269	392,802	(c)	1,046,875
Mexico	4,817	6,599	3,271	3,078	2,191	5,362	1,913	(c)	27,281
Central America	105	44	368	449	95	210	462	876	2,810
South America	531	856	3,579	1,224	1,396	928	2,304	1,844	12,162
West Indies	3,834	12,301	13,528	10,660	9,043	13,957	29,042	5,873	98,088
Total America	11,564	33,424	62,469	74,720	166,597	403,726	426,523	7,593	1,186,616

Alien Passengers from October 1, 1820, to December 31, 1867, and Immigrants from January 1, 1868, to June 30, 1892.

(a) Includes Wales and Great Britain not specified. According to William J. Bromwell's *History of Emigration to the United States*, published in 1866 by Redfield of New York, 1,000,000 of this number were from Ireland, which is probably accurate. During and after the Irish famine large numbers of Irish who could not find money for the passage to the United States did find it possible to go to England to work in coal mines, factories, and in seasonal agricultural employment; the money secured from which enabled them to embark for the United States from various English ports, which explains Bromwell's estimate.

(b) Includes 777 from Azores and 5 from Greenland.

(c) Immigrants from British North American Possessions and Mexico are not included since July 1, 1885.

Author's Note: Official statistics of immigration to the United States began in 1819, so that statements as to the number of aliens arriving prior to that time are largely guesswork.

The "panic" of 1893 had the effect to turn the alien tide the other way—back to Europe. Official statistics as to aliens returning from the United States were not required by law until 1908.

The quarter of a century which has passed since the character of alien arrivals to the United States began turning in the forties, changed so markedly in the decade of 1881 to 1890, is not long enough for accurate analysis of the economic, political and social influence on the United States of the coming of these newer races, so that the statistical records here given do not extend beyond 1892.

THE GERMANS IN THE
MAKING OF AMERICA

THE GERMANS IN THE MAKING OF AMERICA

CHAPTER I

Early German Immigration — Germans in the
Jamestown Settlement — Massachusetts Bay
Colony.

GOVERNOR Horatio Seymour pointed out the
diversity of origin of the American people during
the Revolution in these words:

"Nine men prominent in the early history of
New York and of the Union represent the same
number of nationalities. Schuyler was of Holland, Herkimer of German, Jay of French, Livingston of Scotch, Clinton of Irish, Morris of
Welsh and Hoffman of Swedish descent. Hamilton was born in one of the English West India
Islands, and Baron Steuben, who became a citizen
of New York after the Revolution, was a
Prussian."

In his Memorial Day address, on May 30,
1916, at Arlington Cemetery, President Wilson

said: "America is made up of the nations of the world. Look at the roster of the Civil War. Not recently, but from the first, America has drawn her blood and her impulse from all the sources of energy that spring at the fountains of every race. . . . We have no criticism for men who love the places of their birth and the sources of their origin. We do not wish them to forget their mothers and their fathers, running back through long laborious generations, who have taken part in building up of the strength and spirit of other nations."

While paying due respect to those influences that came from the Puritan settlements, the great achievements in Manhattan and Pennsylvania, the first protest against human slavery by the German Quakers in 1688, the calling of the first Colonial Congress by Governor Jacob Leisler in 1690, the epochal contest for the freedom of the press by Zenger, the explorations of Hendrick Christiansen in New York,[1] and the cultural and economic

---

[1] "The Susquehanna Valley had been visited by Europeans several years before the Pilgrim Fathers made their landing at Plymouth. When Captain Christiansen, the sturdy Dutch navigator, in 1614, selected Albany as the site of a trading post and erected near there a fort, he acted on knowledge already acquired concerning its relation to those routes into the Indian country which converged near the confluence of the Mohawk and the Hudson." Halsey, 32. Christiansen's deserts have never been adequately recognized by historians. He was a Hollander in so far as Holland was still a part of Germany until 1648; but this daring and influential explorer was born in Cleve in the northern part of the Rhine Province, and was therefore a native German.

developments in Pennsylvania — owing much to
the large influx of Germans — laws for the training of children, the useful employments of criminals, and the observance of religious tolerance —
cannot be dismissed as matters of subordinate
interest.   The Dutch had a trading station on
Manhattan before the landing of the Mayflower;
and though Penn's charter of March 5, 1681, was
issued sixty-one years after the landing of the
Pilgrims, "the growth of Pennsylvania was more
rapid than that of any other of the thirteen
colonies, and though it and Delaware, considered
as a unit, were the last founded, save one, it soon
came to rank with the most important, and at the
outbreak of the Revolution, it stood third in population."[2]

When Penn returned from a visit to England in
1699, he found the wilderness of the river valley
dotted with farms.   Here he found not only his
fellow Quakers, but Swedes and Dutch, and Germans from the Rhine, together laying the foundation of a great commonwealth.   The great Palatine immigration which began in 1683 and scattered over the Schuylkill and Lehigh Valleys was
not viewed with favor by the English, who "were
for a time alarmed at the influx of such numbers of

[2] Elson, *United States*, 158; cf. Fiske, *Dutch and Quaker Colonies*,
II, 328-29.

a foreign people; but they were not long in discovering that these Germans were an industrious, peace-loving people, and, while wholly unostentatious, as sincerely religious as the Puritan or the Quaker."[3]

It has been well said by Kapp that the Latins sent to America officers without an army, the Germans sent an army without officers, and the English sent both officers and an army. And it is due to the fact that the great German immigration severed all political connection with the homeland and only maintained a loose family bond, that it became diffused, similarly to the Irish, among the English colonists, and by merging with the already existing political units—supported as these were by a strong European government—it lost the individuality and prestige to which by numbers, culture and enterprise, it was justly entitled. In appraising the value and influence of the various tides of European immigration, we must bear in mind that while everything essential in the history of the English settlements is preserved in the official reports of English governors, proprietaries and commissions to the home government, and these reports have supplied an inexhaustible source of inspiration and material to later-day historians, essayists and poets, few such

---

[3] Elson, *op. cit.*, 158.

records concerning the Germans were preserved in the archives of European governments. In most cases we are assigned to the necessity of going to alien sources for information concerning their activities on the new continent and to be content with the sparing testimony of those who were strangers to them, and not always their well-wishers.

The German settlements had their romance of adventure, of endurance and heroism, no less than had the rocks and hillsides of New England. They formed a far-flung battle line of civilization from Maine to Georgia against Indian raids and depredations. In the French-Indian war and in the war of the Revolution, with the massacres of the Mohawk Valley, Tulpehockon, Northampton County, Reading, and others, too numerous to mention, the Germans bore the brunt. The record is carried on into the early Ohio settlements and down to the last Indian massacre of a white settlement, that of New Ulm, Minnesota, in 1862, in which 178 houses were burned and entire German families were wiped out.

The Teutonic race is inherently a race of naturalists and of land and home seekers, and deep and abiding as is the love of the individual German for his native land, the romantic tendency of his nature, often touched with the idealism of the mystic, has carried him to the remotest corners of the earth in his individualistic capacity, and accounts for traces of his presence in almost all early exploring expeditions.

The first German on American soil was "Tyrker, the German," the discoverer of the grape, noted in the saga of Leif Ericson's expedition to "Wineland" in the eleventh century.[4]

There were a number of Germans among the first English settlers of Jamestown in 1607. Captain John Smith records several in a list of names of the original settlers, Unger, Keffer, etc., and, as Dr. Faust points out, the numerous direct references to the "Dutch" in this connection need not lead us to suppose them to have been natives of Holland, particularly since one is referred to as a "Switzar." Holland in the seventeenth century was the principal embarking point for those going over seas, not only of Dutch citizens, but of people living along the Rhine at points in Germany contiguous to Holland. This circumstance is responsible for some misunderstandings in regard to distinctions between Dutch and Germans, so that almost all persons setting sail from a Dutch port were classed as Hollanders or Dutch.

These "Dutchmen" in the Jamestown colony

---

[4] A. M. Reeves, *Finding of Wineland the Good*, 98; quoted by Faust, *German Element*, I, 6.

were artisans, carpenters mainly, whose services were valuable in a colony, and preferred to "adventurers that never did know what a day's work was, except the Dutchmen and Poles and some dozen others." All the rest, Captain Smith relates, "were poore Gentlemen, Tradesmen, Serving-men, libertines and such like, ten times more fit to spoyle a Commonwealth than either to begin one or but help to maintain one."[5]

"Better far than a batch of average immigrants," writes Dr. Griffis, "was the reinforcement of some German and Polish mechanics, brought over to manufacture glass. These Germans were the first of a great company that have contributed powerfully to build up the industry and commerce of Virginia—'the mother of states and statesmen.' There still stands on the east side of Timber Neck Bay, on the north side of the York River, a stone chimney, with a mighty fireplace, nearly eight feet wide, built by these Germans."[6]

There were Germans in the Massachusetts Bay Colony. Rev. John White, the "patriarch of Dorchester" and the "father of the Massachusetts

---

[5] Faust, op. cit., I, 7-9. In 1620 four millwrights from Hamburg were sent to the same settlement to erect saw mills. Dr. Nicholas Hacke, a native of Cologne, of whom there is mention in 1657, was one of the most highly educated men in early Virginia. Thomas Harmonson, founder of one of the most prominent Eastern Shore families, a native of Brandenburg, was naturalized October 24, 1634.

[6] Romance of American Colonization, 34.

Bay Colony," in the tract attributed to him, *"The Planter's Plea"* (1630), published after the departure of Winthrop's Puritan fleet, writes: "It is not improbable that partly for their sakes, and partly for respect to some Germans that are gone over with them, and more that intend to follow after, even those which otherwise would not much desire innovation of themselves, yet for maintaining of peace and unity (the only solder of a weak, unsettled body), will be won to consent to some variation from the forms and customs of our church."[7]

We may not truthfully assume that the Germans in early American life were merely farmers, laborers and mechanics. Even a hurried survey reveals a number of outstanding names of men of illustrious achievements and of important movements of immigrant bodies of educated Germans, which we shall later undertake to examine at closer range and in greater detail. We shall find that there is little co-relation among these movements except at their source, but that in the aggregate they exerted—particularly in a patriotic, nationalistic sense, to be pointed out in subsequent pages—a vast and material influence on the molding of the national character, and that their contributions to the common task of reclaiming

[7] Lohr,

the virgin soil for civilization and the forming and shaping of American institutions comprise one of the most important pages in the history of the Making of America.

. . . . . .

The history of German immigration begins with the settlement of Germantown, Pennsylvania, under the leadership of Franz Daniel Pastorius in 1683, sixty-one years after the landing of the Pilgrims. The vessel that conveyed to these shores the original thirteen families from Crefeld was the Concord, and the Concord is to the descendants of the first German settlers what the Mayflower is to the descendants of the Pilgrims. The Crefeld colony embarked July 24, 1683, and arrived October 6 of the same year, in Philadelphia.

Pastorius was born September 26, 1651, at Sommernhausen, Franconia. He studied law and lived in Frankfort-on-the-Main. His life is a record of high accomplishments, and he was, not without justice, called the leading scholar of his day in America. No blemish attaches to his character either in his private or public capacity.

On March 4, 1681, a royal charter was issued to William Penn for the province of Pennsylvania, and on March 10, 1682, Penn conveyed to Jacob Telner, of Crefeld, Germany, doing business as a merchant in Amsterdam; Jan Streypers, a mer-

chant of Kaldkirchen, a village near the Dutch
border, and Dirck Sipmann, of Crefeld, each
5,000 acres of land to be laid out in Pennsylvania.
On June 11, 1683, Penn conveyed to Govert
Remke, Lenard Arets, and Jacob Isaac van
Bebber, a baker, all of Crefeld, 1,000 acres of
land each, and they together with Telmer, Strey-
pers and Sipmann, constituted the original Crefeld
purchasers. On July 24th, the Concord, a vessel
of 500 tons, William Jeffries, master, sailed from
Gravesend with the following passengers: Lenard
Arets, Abraham Op den Graeff, Dirck Op den
Graeff, Herman Op den Graeff, William Strey-
pers, Thonas Kunders, Reynier Theissen, Jan
Seimens, Jan Lensen, Peter Keurlis, Johannes
Bleikers, Jan Luckens and Abraham Tunes.

The three Op den Graeffs were brothers. Herman was a son-in-law of Van Bebber; they were
accompanied by their sister Margaretha and their
mother, and they were cousins of Jan and William
Streypers, who also were brothers. The wives of
Thonas Kunders and Lenard Arets were sisters
of the Streypers, and the wife of Jan was the
sister of Reynier Theissen. Peter Keurlis was
also a relative, and the location of Jan Lucken and
Abraham Tunes on the certificate of the marriage
of the son of Thonas Kunders with a daughter of
William Streypers in 1700 indicates that they, too,

were connected with the group by family ties. "It is now ascertained definitely," writes Pennypacker, "that eleven of these thirteen immigrants were from Crefeld, and the presumption that their two companions, Jan Lucken and Abraham Tunes, came from the same city is consequently strong. This presumption is increased by the indications of relationship and the fact that the wife of Jan Seimens was Mercken Williamsen Lucken."[8]

Pastorius had sailed six weeks earlier and had arrived in Philadelphia on August 20, 1683. By the so-called Germantown patent from William Penn he acquired 5,350 acres near Philadelphia and founded Germantown. Acting for his associates, 22,377 additional acres were acquired under the Manatauney Patent, and Germantown was laid out on October 24, 1683.

The principal occupation of the settlers was in the textile industry, farming, and the planting of vineyards. In 1688 Pastorius was elected mayor, and the next year the town was incorporated. He became a member of the Philadelphia schoolboard, was twice elected to the Assembly and also acted as magistrate. Pastorius left a large number of writings in German, English and Latin, which throw much light on the early life of the little settlement and show that

[8] *Settlement of Germantown,* 5.

William Penn was not an infrequent visitor in the hospitable home of the distinguished scholar and pioneers, and that the Quaker proprietor took an earnest interest in the fate of the little colony.

Three famous families issued from Germantown. The Rittenhausens, who established the first paper mill in America and from whom descended the great astronomer and scientist, David Rittenhouse; the Gottfrieds, from whom descended Godfrey, the inventor of the quadrant, and the Sauers, of whom Christoph and his son attained fame as printers and publishers of the first Bible in a European language in America. The ancestor of the Rittenhausens was William (Ruttinghausen), born in 1664 in the principality of Broich, near the city of Mühlheim on the Ruhr, where his brother Heinrich Nicholaus, and his mother Maria Hagerhoffs, were living in 1678. At this time he was a resident of Amsterdam. His ancestors had long been manufacturers of paper at Arnheim, and when he took his oath of citizenship in Amsterdam on June 23, 1678, he was described as a paper maker from Mühlheim. He emigrated to New York, but as there was no printing in that city and no opportunity for carrying on his business of paper making, in 1688, together with his sons, Gerhard and Klaus, and his daughter Elizabeth, who subsequently married

Heivert Papen, he came to Germantown. There, in 1690, on a little stream flowing into the Wissahickon, he erected the first paper mill.[9]

Thomas Kunders' house, 5109 Main street, Germantown, is the only house of the original settlers that can be accurately located to-day. Kunders was a dyer. His death occurred in the fall of 1729. He was the ancestor of the Conard and Conrad families, and among his descendants is Sir Samuel Cunard, founder of the Cunard line of steamships.[10]

Here the first meeting of the Society of Friends in Germantown was held, and it was from the members of this little congregation that the first public protest against human slavery was issued on April 18, 1688. John Greenleaf Whittier has commemorated the event in the following "Lines on reading the message of Governor Ritner of Pennsylvania, in 1836":

And that bold-hearted yeomanry, honest and true,
Who, haters of fraud, gave to labor its due;
Whose fathers of old sang in concert with thine,
On the banks of Swatara the songs of the Rhine, —
The German-born pilgrims, who first dared to brave
The scorn of the proud in the cause of the slave. . .
They cater to tyrants? They rivet the chain,
Which their fathers smote off, on the negro again?

[9] Ibid., 162.
[10] Jenkins, Guide Book to Historic Germantown, 36-37.

Penn's personal interest and friendship for the pilgrims of Germantown is easily explained. Dutch was his native tongue as well as English, as his mother, Margaret Jasper, of Rotterdam, was a native of Holland, and in inviting settlers to come to his province he preached to thousands in the lowlands of Germany, making converts and urging them to come to his Christian Commonwealth. Seidensticker writes: "For more than a century Germantown remained true to its name, a German town. William Penn in 1683 preached there, in Tunes Kunders' house in the German tongue,[11] and General Washington in 1793 attended German service in the Reformed Church."[12]

[11] "Among the languages which he (Penn) could speak fluently were Latin, Italian, French, German and Dutch." Fiske, *Dutch and Quaker Colonies*, II, 115.

[12] Following is a chronology of Germantown events:

1683 August 16, Pastorius reaches Philadelphia.
1683 October 6, Thirteen families from Crefeld reach Philadelphia and settle Germantown.
1688 First protest against slavery issued here.
1690 First paper mill in America established here.
1705 Portrait in oil believed to be the first painted in America, made in Germantown by Dr. Christopher Witt.
1708 First Mennonite meeting house in America built here.
1719 February 17, Death of Pastorius.
1732 April 8, David Rittenhouse born at Germantown.
1743 First Bible in America in a European tongue printed in Germantown by Christopher Sauer.
1760 Germantown Academy founded.
1764 Sauer begins publication of first religious magazine in America.
1770 First American book on pedagogy published.
1772-73 First type ever cast in America made in Germantown. Jenkins, *Guide Book*, 8-9:

"The first settlement consisted of only twelve families of forty-one persons, the greater part High German mechanics and weavers, because I had ascertained that linen cloth would be indispensable. I have also acquired for my High German Company, fifteen thousand acres of land in one piece, on condition that, within a year, they shall actually place thirty households thereon.   It would therefore be a very good thing if the European associates should at once send more persons over here for the common advantage of the Company: for only the day before yesterday the Governor [William Penn] said to me that the zeal of his High Germans in building pleased him very much, and that he preferred them to the English, and would grant them special privileges.". . .

"He [Penn] heartily loves the Germans, and once said openly in my presence to his Councillor and those who were about him, 'I love the Germans and desire that you also should love them'."—Pastorius' *"Circumstantial Geographical Description of Pennsylvania."*

CHAPTER II

Two German Governors of New York, Peter Minnewit and Jacob Leisler — The Palatine Immigration — Various Appraisals of its Importance.

IN the history of the settlements on the North American continent the Germans play a more prominent part in New York and Pennsylvania than in other British colonies; but before we enter into their history as part of the colonial population, we meet with individuals, rather than with considerable groups, impressing themselves upon their times, whose strong personalities stand out in bold relief, and who must be detached from the general mass of incoming Germans, before German immigration can be considered in all its bearings and in its proper place and order. We shall not, therefore, treat of the Palatine immigration into New York until we have briefly disposed of two Germans whose names occupy a fixed place in the record of events connected with early New York.

Washington Irving's *Knickerbocker History of*

New York, published in December, 1809, is chiefly
responsible for a caricature of the Dutch administration of Manhattan Island.   In its pages and in
those of his sketches, the early settlers of the
island, following the discovery of the Hudson in
1609, troop before our vision in the distorted
guise of muddy-pated peasants, unprogressive,
hard-drinking, canny, grasping and cunning; and
their governors human behemoths, more devoted
to their long clay pipes and their tankards than to
the affairs of State, arrantly ignorant and inflated
with stodgy self-conceit.

How greatly Irving departed from the truth in
his avowedly satirical history is fairly illustrated
in the personality of the first governor of New
Netherland, Peter Minnewit, born in Wesel, Germany, on the lower Rhine in 1590, and sent over
by the Dutch West India company in 1626 to take
charge of its trading post.   Minnewit was the son
of wealthy and highly respected parents.   He
studied theology and was elected a deacon
of the Reformed Church in his native town.
He found on his arrival in New Amsterdam
a town of thirty log cabins; and recognizing
his first duty to be the finding of ways and
means of protecting the colonists from Indians
and pirates, he bought the island from the
Indians, erected a stone fort at the southern point,

and surrounded the town with palisades. He stimulated the fur trade and the cultivation of the soil, and built windmills, so that instead of importing flour from Holland, the settlement was soon in a position to export it. Minnewit also cultivated relations of amity with the New England Puritans, and the settlement prospered until the Company in 1629, foolishly, against Minnewit's protest, issued a charter creating the patroon system. The resulting friction led to his recall in 1631 and Minnewit turned to Sweden and later conducted the Swedish colonization project in Delaware, where he died in 1647.

Far from realizing the picture that Irving drew, Minnewit was a man of education, extraordinary intelligence, energy and capacity, and suffers little in comparison with the best English administrators sent over to govern the crown colonies.[1]

Fifty-seven years elapsed before the second German-born governor of New York appeared upon the scene, and political events gave to American history a character of enduring interest in the person of Jacob Leisler. Had his dreams been realized, had he received due support from William III, hailed as their national hero by the Dutch of New Amsterdam, Leisler would have gone

[1] "In his case, as in many others, it has taken centuries to show how exceptional were his services, how unselfish his aims, how rare his judgment, how noble his record." Forsyth, *Beginning of New York*, 13.

down in history as the first great representative
of popular government in New York,[2] as he was
the first martyr to the democratic faith of
America.[3]

Leisler was a native of Frankfort-on-the-Main
and arrived in New York as a soldier in the service of the Dutch West India Company. He
intermarried with the Dutch aristocracy of the
colony and in 1684 was rated the third richest
man on the island, and was appointed a member
of the Admiralty Court of Governor Dongan.
Three things have given him his place in American history: His calling of the first colonial congress, his espousal of the popular cause, and his
political martyrdom.

Leisler became the central figure of a state of
acute political disturbances and confusion following the revolution in England, which dethroned
James II and brought William of Orange to London at the invitation of Parliament, inaugurating
the reign of William and Mary (1689). When
the news arrived of the change of government in
England, Dutch disgust in New York over the
joint administration of New England, New York
and New Jersey under Governor Andros, fanned
the existing discontent into open revolt, and Leis-

---

[2] Cf. Fiske, *Dutch and Quaker Settlements*, II, 207.
[3] Lossing, *Eminent Americans*, 65.

ler was selected as the natural leader, although he at first declined the leadership. He was favored by the Dutch on account of his German birth, his military experience and his wealth and influence with the masses. Public disturbances followed, the mob captured the fort, and on June 8, 1689, the Committee of Safety chose Leisler commander-in-chief of the stronghold and of the city. Leisler sent a messenger to London expressing his loyalty and that of the people of the province, of which he had meanwhile been elected commander-in-chief by the Committee of Safety; but met with little sympathy, as the king's mind had been poisoned against him by Lieutenant Governor Nicholson, Andros' underling. Instead of reaping the reward of his loyalty, Leisler's name was dragged through the mire and he was accused of being a tyrant, usurper, demagogue, Papist and Jacobite.

Opposed to him at home were the colonial aristocrats, the Schuylers, Bleeckers, Van Rensellaers, Cuylers, and the Tories. Complete quiet was not restored until the arrival of a royal messenger in December, 1689, with a letter addressed to Francis Nicholson, "or in his absence to such as for the time being take care for Preserving the Peace and administering the Lawes in our Province." Leisler adopted the title of lieutenant-governor and appointed a council of nine from the various trades of the province. This course resulted in a period of tranquillity; but hardly had Leisler become master of his enemies than the French sent the Indians into New York under Frontenac and destroyed Schenectady, massacring the inhabitants.

In this period fall events destined to figure as precursors of the Continental Congress[4]—the calling of the first congress of the American colonies.

Leisler's invitation calling a conference of the colonies was accepted by the governors of Massachusetts, Plymouth, New Jersey and Maryland; and the congress decided to conquer Canada, each colony agreeing to furnish a quota of fighting men and Massachusetts additionally to equip a fleet for the taking of Quebec. The force was to be augmented by a contingent of 1,800 Mohawk warriors. But owing to jealousy among the leaders, the expedition failed. The only distinction was won by Leisler, who had equipped the first warship that sailed out of the port of New York, added three ships to the fleet, captured six French vessels, which he had condemned and sold as prizes, and by his energy and enterprise proved that he deserved the confidence of his supporters and the respect of his enemies.

But the failure of the expedition outweighed all

---

[4] Fiske, *op. cit.*, 182-184.

consideration of his merits. He was made the scapegoat, and the home government, late in 1690, sent Colonel Henry Sloughter to New York. as Governor. Leisler, having refused to surrender control of the fort and city to Major Richard Ingolsby—who had arrived before Sloughter— until presented with proper credentials, was arrested, tried before a commission composed of his personal enemies, and together with his son-in-law, Milborne, convicted of high treason. Their death warrant was signed by Sloughter, and Leisler and Milborne were hanged on a spot, at the corner of the present Pearl and Center streets, not far from the Tombs.

The act was later disapproved. In 1695 by an act of Parliament, Leisler's name was exonerated and honored, indemnity was paid to his heirs, and the remains of these victims of judicial murder were honorably buried within the edifice of the Reformed Church. No unprejudiced historian can but esteem Leisler, the lover of union and the champion of the people's rights.[5]

. . . .

Two decades intervene between the death of

---

[5] Griffis, *Romance of American Colonization*, 228, Fiske, *D. and Q. Colonies*, 207. Gouverneur Morris of New York was a lineal descendant through two of Leisler's daughters. Morris was a member of the convention to draft the Constitution, as was Gen. Frederick Frelinghuysen, a grandson of Rev. Theodore J. Frelinghuysen, who was born within the present borders of Prussia. Faust II, 125.

Leisler and the first great inrush of Leisler's countrymen, and we here enter upon an era of British colonization rich in those experiences that furnish the romance of American border history, though it is the romance of a desperate struggle for survival, of official deceit and betrayal, in which the white claimant of the soil stands humiliated in contrast with the generosity of the native red-skin.

Early American historians, diarists and writers betrayed a strong tendency to ignore the cultural labor of the German element and refer to the Palatines in Pennsylvania and New York as "ignorant and superstitious,"[6] and this tendency has been perpetuated by some modern writers.[7] Macaulay appraised them more benevolently when he said that they were "honest, laborious men who had once been thriving burghers of Heidelberg or Mannheim, or who had cultivated vineyards on the banks of the Neckar and the Rhine. . . . Their ingenuity and their diligence

[6] Fiske: "The earlier writers on American history were apt to ignore or pass over in silence the contributions to American civilization that have been made by other people than the English. Perhaps this may have been because our earliest historians were men of New England whose attention was unduly occupied with their own neighborhood. At all events there can be no doubt of the fact. The non-English element in our composite were not so much denied as disregarded, like infinitesimals in algebra." *Dutch and Quaker Colonies*, I, 30.

[7] Lodge, *English Colonies*, 228; Parkman, *Montcalm and Wolfe*, I, 31, and *Conspiracy of Pontiac*, II, 84; Lamb, *City of New York*, I, 485.

could not fail to enrich any land which should afford them an asylum."[8]   A close student of the Palatines in New York, Sanford H. Cobb, expresses a high estimate of them in these words: "The Story of the Palatines challenges our sympathy, admiration, and reverence, and is as well worth telling as that of any other colonial immigration.   You may concede that their influence on the future development of the country and its institutions was not equal to the formative power exerted by some other contingents.   Certainly, they have not left so many broad and deep marks upon our history as have the Puritans of New England, and yet their story is not without definite and permanent monuments of beneficence towards American life and institutions.   At least one among the very greatest of the safeguards of American liberty—the Freedom of the Press—is distinctly traceable to the resolute boldness of a Palatine."[9]

And most admonitory are the words of Judge Benton: "The particulars of this Palatine or German immigration, . . . seem worthy of extended notice.   The events which produced the movement in the heart of an old and polished European nation, and the causes which prompted these

[8] *Works*, IV, 81.
[9] *Palatines*, 5.

people to seek a refuge and home on the western continent, are quite as legitimate a subject of local American history, as the oft-repeated relation of the exodus of the Pilgrim fathers from Europe, and their landing at Plymouth Rock."[10]

[10] *Herkimer County*, 8.

CHAPTER III

Germans in New York—Sent to the Hudson by
Queen Anne—Their Treatment by Governor
Hunter—A Desperate Situation—The Exodus
—Indian Friends—Palatine Worthies; Weiser,
Zenger, Herkimer.

WHEN England had taken possession of the
Atlantic coast from the St. Lawrence to the
Savannah, she broadened her policy of colonization. Either the government or interested groups
of persons defrayed the expenses of transportation and frequently the first cost of settlement.
The first Palatines who in collective units found
their way to London, trusting to fortune for their
subsistence because they had nothing to hope for
at home, comprised 61 persons from Landau under their Pastor, Kocherthal. To the number of
52 survivors, they set sail from England the
middle of October 1708, with the newly-appointed
governor of New York, Lord Lovelace, and
landed in New York during the closing days of the
year. They were sent up the Hudson and were
allotted lands on the west side of the stream,

where they founded Neuburg—the Newburgh of the present day.

The news of the welcome extended to the Palatines reached Germany in exaggerated reports; thousands began their journey down the Rhine and waited at Rotterdam to be shipped to England where Queen Anne had offered them asylum. By the middle of October, 1709, approximately 14,000 Palatines and Swabians had collected in London and were supported by the Queen from her private exchequer and by public subscriptions. Of this number 3,800, including all the linen weavers, were sent into Ireland to develop the Irish linen industry and incidentally to fortify Protestantism, and were there supported by an annual subsidy of 8,000 pounds. Almost 1,000 died in the camps, and it was decided to send to the American colonies many of the thousands that remained; accordingly, 650 were shipped to North Carolina and more than 3,000, in April, 1710, to New York.

Lord Lovelace having died, his successor as governor of New York was Colonel Robert Hunter (September, 1709). He received orders to take the Germans and settle them along the Hudson and Mohawk rivers. Hunter sailed in April, 1710, and reached New York on June 13. The Palatines were distributed among ten vessels, among them the Lyon and the frigates Herbert and Berkeley Castle. According to the governor, more than 470 persons died during the journey, and 250 more soon after landing. The casualties amounted to 20 per cent. Those that survived made a total of 2,227 souls, and they were not allowed to enter the city for fear of spreading infectious diseases, but were temporarily housed on Governor's Island. Huts and tents were put up for their accommodation during the spring; the city sent physicians and medicines, and nature did the rest. The epidemic was soon checked, but 250 had perished on the island, and of those who survived, about 400 scattered in New York during the summer. At least one of these survivors became a prominent figure at a later day and lived to exercise a momentous influence in establishing the principle of the freedom of the press. The remainder of the Palatines were sent up the Hudson to settle the lands selected for that purpose.

The history of the Newburgh settlement was replete with tragic incidents. The Germans were soon to discover that the hospitality shown them was not without onerous reservations. Little by little they were dispossessed of the major part of their allotments, and, under the encroachment of English settlers, their 500 acres of church-lands presented to them by the Crown passed, by trickery, into the possession of the Church of England; many intermarried, others removed to Pennsylvania and to the settlements on the Schoharie and the Mohawk, and presently the earliest Palatine settlement was only a memory.

The later comers passed through even more harrowing vicissitudes; their history forms a vital part of the history of America. With the advent of Governor Hunter—a former soldier of humble origin and a true type of the British climber, regarding the foreign-born as pariahs[1]—the settlers were destined to experience the severest cruelty and hardships. The guiding motive in bringing the Germans to New York had been to render England independent of other countries for her needed supply of naval stores, turpentine, tar, resin and timber. With this in view, Hunter selected a section along the Hudson rich in fir but with a hopelessly sterile soil unfit for cultivation, and moved the German settlers on to the land in September and October, 1710, dividing them into two camps on both sides of the river, about two miles south of Catskill.

Two years at least would be required to prepare the trees to yield their harvest of turpentine and tar, during which the settlers had to be supported at the charge of the Crown. Accordingly,

[1] Cf. Kapp, *Deutschen im Staate New York*, 33.

the Palatines arriving late in the fall of 1710 could neither be put to the work for which they had been imported nor begin to cultivate the soil and make their homesteads. Under the prolonged idleness in their cramped quarters, discontent, envy and friction ensued, which were added to by disgust with the unsavory food supplied under contract by Robert Livingston. The men complained that they had come to secure land for themselves and their children and to make themselves independent by establishing homesteads. The parcels allotted to them were insufficient. They claimed they had promises of larger and better tracts from the Indians on the Schoharie, which was true.

About the middle of May, 1711, the general discontent burst into open flame. The Palatines refused to continue their labors, declining especially to be further concerned with the work of producing tar, drove out the surveyors and formed an oath-bound federation to stand together and move to the Schoharie, with or without the governor's consent.

Hunter sent to Albany for soldiers, the insurrection was quelled, and passed off without bloodshed.

For a time all went well, and in the unsuccessful expedition to Canada it was resolved to add to the "350 Christians and 150 Indians from Long Island, 500 Palatines," which number they supplied readily. Their position was little better than that of slaves, however, and with the mismanagement of the pine lands, the increasing deficits and growing friction between Hunter and the settlers, many of the latter deserted and turned to Pennsylvania and the Schoharie. After a few years they were finally abandoned to their fate by Hunter's voluntary renunciation of his authority. The enterprise had proved a complete failure.

Left to their own devices and confirmed in their possessions by crown patents, the Palatines soon prospered. They had founded Hunterstown, Kingsbury, Annsberg, Haysburg, Rhinebeck, Newtown, Georgetown, Elizabethtown, Kingstown and Esopus. Hunter in releasing them from their contracts had left them without resources and cast them entirely upon their own ingenuity and industry, so that while many remained on the Hudson, many took up their residence on the Schoharie.

The tribulations of the latter are graphically summed up in a letter of complaint to the Crown, dated in August, 1722:

"It was toward the end of the year (1712), with winter, so severe in this country, at the door. Food was not to be had, and clothing was even lacking to cover our bare nakedness. This news created general consternation among the settlers, and women and children burst into agonizing complaints and execrations such as perhaps have never been uttered by poor people before. Thus, against our will, we were subjected to the harsh necessity of asking protection of the Indians. The latter had on a former occasion presented to Queen Anne a strip of land called Schoharie to be divided among us; but all appeals to Hunter to allow us to settle there had been refused. Although belonging to the Palatines, he claimed he could not permit them to go, as he had not enough men to garrison the section for their protection. Now some leaders were dispatched to the Indians, who gave them an account of our desperate plight. Abandoned by the governor and without means to go elsewhere, they begged their Indian friends to let them settle at Schoharie. They received them kindly and granted their prayer with the remark that they had presented the land to Queen Anne with the explicit understanding that it was to be divided among the Palatines. Nothing should now prevent them from taking possession of it, and they, the Indians, would aid them to the full extent of their power. When the leaders returned with this cheerful message, new courage filled the hearts of the settlers. They eagerly seized the offered opportunity, and in less than two weeks, in spite of hunger and distress, they cut a road through the forest fifteen miles long. At first they sent fifty families to Schoharie, where, immediately after their arrival they were overtaken by the governor's message that they would not be permitted to settle there and that whoever acted contrary to his orders would be treated as a rebel. These words sounded like thunder in their ears. But the Palatines had carefully considered the grounds for and against their step, and, convinced that they could not make their living anywhere else, they resolved, with starvation staring them in the face, rather to expose themselves to the wrath of the governor than to return. In March of the year 1713 the remainder followed. The snow lay three feet deep; the travelers had to contend with hunger and cold, but after 14 days on the road they at last reached the promised land, Schoharie. The number of Germans that settled there was too large for the land which the Indians had granted them for the support of their wives and children. Some citizens of Albany tried to buy up the surrounding land in order to isolate the Palatines by these means. But the Indians gave the latter the preference and sold them the surrounding lands for $300. But scarcely had Governor Hunter heard of this transaction between the Indians and the Germans, than he sought, through one Adam Vrooman, to induce the Indians to break the contract. The misery which these poor half-starved people suffered during their first settlement at Schoharie is almost incredible, and if the Indians in their kindness had not shown them the places where they could obtain some edible plants and roots, they must have perished of starvation, one and all. What God in His wrath had said to Adam, 'Thou shalt eat of the grass of the fields,' was literally fulfilled as to them."[2]

The German immigrants had reached their destination only with what they wore and could carry in their hands. Because of Hunter's disapproval of their course they had not been per-

[2] *Ibid.*, 55.

mitted to take any of their tools, implements or supplies, and having arrived in the valley, they lived, half naked, in rude cabins, calculated to protect them only against the severest cold. They were without horses or cows. Their first plows consisted of large scythes; the first corn they were able to harvest from their lands was ground into flour between stones. In the fall of 1713 Lambert Sternberg carried the first bushel of wheat 19 miles on his back from Schenectady, and within the confines of a tumble-down hedge of an abandoned Indian camp it was sown for protection against the weather, and flourished handsomely.

Forty years later these settlers annually sent to Albany 36,000 bushels of wheat. The interval is a record of privations and hardships such as few, if any, American settlements can duplicate. For many years groups of from 15 to 20 men, combined for protection against wild beasts, had to visit Schenectady to have their wheat ground, each carrying a bushel or more in weight; and it was not until the middle of the century that William Fuchs built the first mill on Fox Creek and thus cut the distance by more than half. Their clothing consisted of deer-skins supplied by the Indians. When and how they obtained the first cows and pigs is not recorded, but there is an explicit account of the first horse bought at Schenectady by nine citizens of Weisersdorf. It was an old gray mare, and the poor animal was alternately used one day by each owner, from week to week.

Their nearest neighbors were the Indians and the Dutch. The former a branch of the Mohawks, were their steady friends and assisted them in any way possible. And the settlers were wise enough to cultivate their friendship and sympathy. Their leader and spokesman was Johann Conrad Weiser, destined to be the progenitor of a distinguished line of descendants.

The prosperity of the Schoharie settlement, relates Faust, aroused the cupidity of the earlier settlers, who now became actively engaged in reviving Governor Hunter's grudge against the Palatines. Overstepping his prerogatives, the governor granted to the Seven Partners of Albany at a very moderate price the identical lands on which the Palatines had settled, obviously designing to drive the Germans out of the fertile valley, choosing to forget the original instructions of Queen Anne, according to which he was to engage them in the business of producing naval stores, but also to have special concern for the "comfort and advantage of the Palatines."

The Seven Partners (one of them was Robert Livingston, Jr.) soon sent an agent named Bayard to acquaint the Germans with the new order of things, and offered them the lands they had cultivated at a small rental. When his purpose became known, men, women and children, armed with clubs, sickles, knives and guns, appeared before the house in Schmidtsdorf where Bayard was staying, and but for his host, Schmidt, who harangued the people until Bayard could make his escape, the agent would have been hardly used. The Seven Partners then sent Sheriff Adams to renew the offer and drive from the land those who should be unwilling to accept their terms, especially Weiser. According to the sheriff's own account, he was struck down in the act of seizing one of the insurgents, dragged through all the filthy pools of the streets by the women of the village, then set upon a fence-rail and carried about for an hour. He lost an eye and had two of his ribs broken, but managed, four days later, to reach Albany. When, after some time of watchful waiting, a group of the bolder young men, including young Weiser, went to Albany for salt, they were arrested and thrown into jail, from which they were eventually released because of insufficient evidence involving them in the sheriff's discomfiture.

Being unable to dislodge the Palatines, the Seven Partners next applied to the governor, and that worthy summoned three men from each of the seven villages to appear before him at Albany, including the elder Weiser, whom, in a burst of passion, he threatened to hang; and, his orders having been obeyed, he inquired, first, why they had gone to Schoharie without his permission; secondly, why they would not compromise with the gentlemen of Albany, and finally, why they had so much to do with the Indians.

To this they answered that they had been compelled by necessity to shift for themselves, the governor having told them to do so when the manufacture of naval stores was discontinued. They were compelled to go somewhere to escape starvation, hoping later to gain the approval of the king and of the governor. At the mention of the king, Hunter waxed angry, and Livingston added, "Here is your king," pointing to Hunter.

To the second question the deputies replied that they had no dealings with the gentlemen of Albany, that the Indians had presented the land to the crown for the benefit of the Palatines and that they had bought the additional lands from the Indians; that the king had not given it to the Seven Partners. They would serve the king but no private person.

Their answer to the third question was that if they did not live on good terms with the Indians, they would constantly be exposed to hostile attacks both from the French and the Indians.

Hunter commanded them either to agree with the Albany gentlemen or to leave the valley, and forbade them to plow and sow the land until they had come to an agreement. When subsequent petitions to the governor proved unavailing, the Palatines in the Spring of 1718 decided to appeal to a higher power, meanwhile stubbornly holding their lands and "sowing some small corn and fruits, as else they must have starved," declared Weiser.

They decided to send three envoys to London to argue their case. The three, the elder Weiser, Scheff and Wallrath, secretly boarded a ship at Philadelphia; but only a few days out the vessel was boarded by pirates, the passengers robbed of all their money, Weiser lashed three times to the mast and flogged to extort more money from him; and thus impoverished, friendless and unknown, they reached London. Compelled to contract debts which they were unable to pay, Weiser and Scheff were cast into prison and remained confined there a whole year before they received a check for 70 pounds from home and obtained their release. Wallrath had started for home before he could be arrested and died on his homeward journey.

The two envoys ably presented their case before the Lords of Trade in separate petitions.
The documents prove their authors to have been
men of education, casting a far more favorable
light on the intellectual average of the Palatines
than is generally accorded them. Though supported by both pastors of the Royal German
Chapel in London, the envoys failed to effect a
satisfactory solution of their difficulties, Hunter
himself testifying adversely to their claim, and
Scheff, disagreeing with Weiser's plan of threatening that the Palatines would leave the province
of New York and settle in Pennsylvania if their
petitions were not granted, separated from
Weiser and returned home alone. In 1722
Weiser still tarried in London, determined to
obtain a favorable decision for the Palatines if
such a thing were possible, but in 1723 he was
again in Schoharie.

He found the people discussing three courses:
To remain in Schoharie after coming to an
agreement with the Seven Partners; to settle in
the Mohawk Valley on land assigned them by the
new governor, Burnet, or to start a migration
to the neighboring colony of Pennsylvania. Burnet proving a more tactful official than his prede-
cessor, an understanding was reached by which
about 300 persons remained at Schoharie under

favorable circumstances, these being afterwards joined by additional settlers from Germantown and Rhinebeck, so that the whole of the Schoharie country was largely settled by Germans at the time of the Revolution. They extended their farms for 25 to 30 miles beyond the original seven villages. They turned the wilderness into a garden, and though described by Governor Burnet in a moment of pique as "a laborious and honest, but headstrong and ignorant people," they rendered valuable service and were active in the frontier struggles and in the war of the Revolution.

Under their leader, Gerlach, other Palatines settled in the Mohawk Valley in the present counties of Montgomery, Herkimer and beyond. The entire distance between Frankfort and Schenectady is 70 miles, of which the Germans settled more than two-thirds. In this location, Dr. Faust points out, they protected the frontier of New York throughout the French and Indian and Revolutionary wars, the Schoharie Germans forming the side of the wedge running into the western territory of New York. The district soon became the richest grain section in time of peace and war, and the work of Governor Burnet was well rewarded. In number the Palatine settlers of the Mohawk Valley, about the middle of the eighteenth century, aggregated from 2,500 to 3,000, inhabiting about 500 houses. Indian traders advanced as far as Oswego and Niagara, which marked the border also of the Six Nations. Even to-day the Mohawk Valley is Palatine territory, indexed with German names, as Palatine, Palatine Bridge, Mannheim, Oppenheim, Newkirk, etc. The meadows extending along the south side of the Mohawk, unsurpassed in cultivation and fertility, are still known as the German Flatts. On the opposite side of the Mohawk lies the town bearing the name of General Herkimer, the hero of the Battle of Oriskany.

The elder Weiser decided upon a course similar to Gerlach's, refused to bend his neck to the Albany landlords, and chose rather to abandon the lands that he and his people had cultivated for 12 years and made habitable. Encouraged by Governor Keith of Pennsylvania, who had promised to protect their liberties against injustice such as they suffered from the British governor of New York, a group of settlers decided to buy a section of land that was set aside for them at Tulpehocken, and two expeditions set out, the first in the Spring of 1723, the second in 1728.

About 60 families of 300 persons left Scoharie. They were no longer the poor outcasts of the period of 1714, but formed a caravan with

numerous cattle and abundant supplies and money
to make a good beginning. Following the Schoharie, they crossed the mountains in a south-
westerly direction to the headwaters of the
Susquehannah under the guidance of an Indian,
built canoes with which they navigated the river
to the mouth of the Swatara, ascended the latter
stream and reached the undulating country between the sources of the Swatara and Tulpehock-
en. Here they founded their first settlement of
Heidelberg and then sent word back to Schoharie
of the success of their expedition.

Weiser had tarried behind in the stubborn hope
of still getting a clear title to the lands in New
York; and disappointed at last, he led his people,
five years later, to Pennsylvania, founding the
town of Womelsdorf, which rapidly gained in importance. Here the younger Weiser first came
into notice and was soon recognized as a man of
affairs in the settlements of Berks County. As a
soldier, pathfinder and mediator with the Indians
his fame spread throughout the land, and in his
home the elder Weiser lived almost a score of
years longer, his closing days gladdened with the
vision of prosperity and increase all about, and
peace at last. "He had been one of the most
stubborn fighters for justice and independence in

all colonial history," writes Dr. Faust,[3] an estimate that is not exaggerated, in view of his determined stand against Hunter and the defense of his
people's rights before the very throne of Great
Britain, undaunted by poverty, violence, imprisonment and the law's delay.

The great Palatine exodus whose tide was
directed to the new world thereafter carefully
avoided New York.[4] The stories told of the in-
dignities inflicted upon their countrymen along the
Hudson and Schoharie, and their terrible sufferings, turned the eyes of the new venturers to
Pennsylvania. Within 20 years of the settlement
of Tulpehocken, the Germans in the Pennsylvania
counties had increased to nearly 50,000.

.   .   .   .   .   .

Even after the affairs of the settlers with their
white oppressors had been adjudicated, they were
still to pass through the period of Indian depreda-

[3] *German Element,* I, 104.
[4] This is true in general; an exception is recorded in the *New York
Gazette* of October 8, 1764, where it is stated: "At a time when by a
new System of Regulations in Commerce, our Trade is oppressed and
restrained, and our Spirits sunk to as low an Ebb, as by natural Consequences our Purses must be bye and bye, Providence seems to aleviate
our Pains, by sending Peter Hasenclever, a public and noble-spirited
Stranger amongst us, who last week introduced into this Province, at an
immense Expense, above 200 Germans (women included), consisting all
of artificers, as Miners, Founders, Forgers, Colliers, Wheelwrights, Carpenters, etc.   There never was brought a finer or more valuable set of
people to America than these." *Iconography of Manhattan Island, The
Revolutionary Period,* 1763-1776.   In truth, Hasenclever's industrial
colonization scheme was almost as important as the earlier Palatine
movement.   See Cronau, *German Achievements,* 34.

tions during the Revolution. The story of the invasion of the Schoharie Valley by Sir John Johnson and his Indian ally, Joseph Brant, as related by Kapp, is among the most revolting recitals of war. Murder, arson and pillage continued even after the surrender of Cornwallis. The Indians and the Tories destroyed in a few hours what had cost years of toil. Many German settlers were shot dead in their fields, ambushed on the way home from work, their women and children scalped or dragged into captivity.

Brant began operations in July, 1778, surprising a little settlement of only seven families at Andrustown, Herkimer County, killing two and dragging the women away as prisoners. This was followed by an attack on German Flatts, a settlement of about 1,000 people, who having been warned, fled to the two forts. The attack resulted in the destruction of 63 houses, 57 barns, three flour and two saw mills, and the loss of 235 horses, 229 head of cattle, 269 sheep and 93 oxen. In June, 1778, Brant destroyed Cobelskill; a local company of defenders under Captain Braun was ambushed and practically annihilated; 23 were killed and others seriously wounded, and only six escaped, while the women fled into the woods and from there watched the Indians set fire to their houses. From here Brant and the Tories turned to the Wyoming Valley to wreak their vengeance, and in July attacked the Mohawk Valley. In August 1779 General Sullivan and General Clinton moved against the Six Nations and destroyed more than 40 Indian villages; but the pursuit was not pressed, and as early as the spring of 1780 the redskins reappeared and on April 3 surprised Riemenschneider's Bush, burned the flour mill and carried off 19 prisoners. A scouting party under Lieutenant Woodworth from Fort Dayton fell into an ambush and Woodworth died with more than half his men.

In July 1780, Brant, who had his spies everywhere, learned that General Clinton had sent the troops in Canajoharie to Fort Schuyler to protect the supplies at that place, and on August 2, at the head of 500 Indians and Tories, he suddenly hurled himself upon Canajoharie and instituted a terrible massacre. Sixteen men lay dead where they had been shot down, 60 women and children were taken captive, the church, 63 houses with their barns and stables, were reduced to ashes and upward of 300 head of cattle driven off or killed. All the agricultural implements and tools were destroyed, preventing the survivors even from gathering their ripening crops.

In October the British officer Johnson with 1,000 Indians attacked the forts, but all the settlers had been warned and were able to reach the forts before the blow fell. The attacks were beaten off, but Sir John's disappointment found vent in destroying everything in the valley. Hardly a house, barn or hayrick remained. A fierce north wind fanned the flames which destroyed 300 houses and barns; all the livestock was driven off and even the church at Middleburg was burned. All that remained were a few houses belonging to Tories. When the settlers after Johnson's retreat ventured forth from the forts, all they found of their former earthly goods was a heap of smoking ruins.

These compass the main events of this character but by no means exhaust them. They turned many a heart into stone, and long after no Indian or Tory was safe from attack.

.   .   .   .   .   .

The three most prominent names connected with the Palatine settlements in New York are those of the Weisers, General Herkimer and John Peter Zenger. To Conrad Weiser and Herkimer we shall refer later. The last of the trio was the central figure of the great legal contest for the freedom of the press in America, conducted with consummate skill and great eloquence in behalf of Zenger by the great Philadelphia lawyer, Andrew

Hamilton, a native of Ireland.[5] This is one of the great cases that decided the liberties of the people and established the principle afterwards embodied in one of the amendments to the Constitution. Zenger was one of the 400 left behind in New York City when the remainder of the hard-tried Palatines were sent up the Hudson to produce turpentine and other British naval stores under Governor Hunter. He had the good fortune when still a boy to be indentured to Bradford, the printer, to learn the printer's trade and fit himself for editorial work as Bradford's assistant. Unable to conform longer to the policy of Bradford's paper in upholding the repressive, arbitrary acts of the provincial government, he established the *New York Weekly Journal*, November 5, 1733, and began to question Governor Cosby's infractions, interference with juries, etc., in a series of scathing criticisms, leading to his arrest in 1735 by order of the governor. For personal reasons the governor in that year removed the chief justice of the colony from office.

Placed on trial for criminal libel, described in the Attorney General's complaint as " a seditious Person, and a frequent Printer and Publisher of false News and seditious Libels," and charged

---

[5] Kapp, *op. cit.*, 188, says he was a native of Ireland; other authorities assert he was born in Scotland.

specifically that he "did falsely, seditiously and scandalously print and publish . . . a certain false, malicious, seditious, scandalous Libel . . . concerning His Excellency the said Governour . . . [in which publication he represented a former inhabitant explaining that he had left the colony, as he doubts not others will, because, among other reasons] They . . . think . . . that their Liberties and Properties are precarious, and that Slavery is like to be intailed on them and their Posterity, if some past Things are not amended . . . [and] we see mens deeds destroyed, judges arbitrarily displaced, new courts erected without the consent of the Legislature . . . who . . . then . . [can] call . . . any Thing his own, or enjoy any Liberty . . . longer than those in the Administration . . . will condescend to let them do it. . . ."[6]

Zenger was vigorously prosecuted and as ably defended. In his own words: "The Jury withdrew and in a small time returned, and being asked by the Clerk, Whether they were agreed of their Verdict, and whether John Peter Zenger was guilty of Printing and Publishing the Libels in the Information mentioned? They answered by Thomas Hunt, their Foreman, 'Not Guilty.' Upon which there were three Huzzas in the Hall

[6] Rutherford, *John Peter Zenger*, 64.   West, Source Book, 352.

which was crowded with People, and the next Day I was discharged from my imprisonment."

Gouverneur Morris styled the acquittal of the daring editor "the morning star of that liberty which subsequently revolutionized America."[7]

[7] It is interesting to note that Woodrow Wilson in his *American People*, II, 56, miscalls Zenger's name "Ziegler"—John Peter Ziegler—and dismisses the case with a colorless paragraph.

CHAPTER IV

The Germans in Pennsylvania—Misjudged by
Franklin—Ignorance was General and not Con-
fined to the Germans—Their Number—Their
Industry Praised by Foreigners — The "Royal
Americans."

How many Germans landed at the port of
Philadelphia previously to the passage of the
Registration act of 1727 is not known, but all
authorities are agreed that the number was large.
As early as 1717 the volume of German immigration attracted attention and excited the alarm of
the Provincial Government, so that in that year
the Provincial Assembly passed the Registration
law, compelling all immigrants to register and
swear allegiance to the King of Great Britain and
fidelity to the Proprietary of the Province. The
German immigrants had large families and soon
constituted a formidable element of the population. Deputy Governor Thomas expressed the
opinion that in 1747 the province had 120,000 inhabitants, of which three-fifths, or 72,000, were
Germans. Franklin in 1776 credited the province

with 160,000 colonists, of whom one-third, or 53,000, were Germans and one-third Quakers. Diffenderfer is of the opinion that there were between 90,000 and 100,000 Germans in Pennsylvania when the Revolutionary war broke out. Faust estimates them at 110,000.[1]

The large influx of these strangers was not viewed with favor, and Benjamin Franklin, although he had close association with Germans, published a number of German books and was interested in the publication of a German newspaper, expressed fear that they would eventually outnumber his own people. "Of the six Printing-Houses in the Province, two are entirely German, two half German, half English, and but two entirely English. . . . The Signs in our Streets have Inscriptions in both Languages, and in some places only German. . . . In short, unless the Stream of their Importation could be turned from this to other Colonies, . . . they will soon so outnumber us, that all the advantage we have, will not in my Opinion be able to preserve our Language, and even our Government will become precarious."[2]

[1] Cf. post, p. 115.
[2] Letter to Richard Jackson, Philadelphia, May 5, 1753, *Writings* (Smith ed.), III, 140. In the same letter Franklin speaks of the Germans in Pennsylvania being "generally the most ignorant stupid sort of their own Nation," and in 1755 in an address to the British public he asks why should the Palatine boors be suffered to swarm in our settlements. Speaking of the Scotch, Franklin told Arthur Lee that they "who in many places were numerous, were secret or open foes, as opportunity

Some years later Franklin seems to have changed his opinion; he described them as "a people who brought with them the greatest wealth —industry and integrity, and characters that have been superpoised and developed by years of suffering and persecution."

For a time it was actually proposed to pass laws restricting German immigration, and in 1738 Deputy-Governor Thomas, addressing the Council in regard to such a proposed measure, felt impelled to use the following emphatic language:

This Province has been for some years the Asylum of the distressed Protestants of the Palatinate, and other parts of Germany, and I believe it may with truth be said that the present flourishing condition of it is in a great measure owing to the Industry of those People; and should any discouragement divert them from coming hither, it may well be apprehended that the value of your lands will fall, and your Advances to wealth be much slower.[*]

In no colony were the Germans treated better than in that of Pennsylvania; and the misuse of the Palatines by Governor Hunter and the

offered." *Life of Arthur Lee*, by Richard Henry Lee, I, 343. Franklin for a time at least was obviously a "nativist." George F. Baer, in an address entitled, "Germans in Pennsylvania," in 1895, says: "It is highly probable that Franklin's judgment of the Germans was warped by political considerations. He was a New Englander by birth. Prior to the Revolution he was a consistent Royalist. . . . The Germans owed no allegiance to Great Britain and were therefore regarded as a foreign element, capable by throwing their fortunes with either of the European powers contending for the supremacy in America, of seriously affecting the interests of Great Britain."

[*] *Pennsylvania Colonial Records*, IV, 315.

colonial barons of New York having become
noised about through the German states, the tide
of immigration turned from New York to Philadelphia and thence spread out over the colony,
settling principally the counties of Lancaster,
Berks, Bucks, Lebanon, York, Lehigh and Northampton. This was the origin of the "Pennsylvania Dutch." When Washington during the
war of liberation spoke of "my loyal Dutch belt,"
we are justified to infer that he did not allude
exclusively to the loyal Hollanders along the Hudson, but that his encomium embraced their relatives, the German settlers in New York, New
Jersey and Pennsylvania.

The majority of these Germans became well-
to-do. The Pennsylvania farmer belonged, as a
rule, to the substantial, permanent, and best class
of freeholders. "They were, for the period, scientific and economical farmers, and thoroughly well
off, which was especially the case with the Germans, who were thrifty, temperate, never in debt,
and whose women-folk labored in the field. . . .
Baron Stiegel's house at Mannheim was built of
imported brick, and had a private chapel, while
over the high wainscots landscapes were painted
or tapestry hung on the walls, and the fireplaces
were decked with porcelain tiles."[4]

[4] Lodge, *English Colonies*, 249, 250.

The charge of ignorance, often brought against the German settlers during colonial days, may as impartially be applied to all other settlers of the period.[5]

Of the British settlers below the gentry class, a large proportion could not write or read, and for many years in most colonies except Massachusetts and Connecticut, there were few schools. The closing years of the 17th century were a period of deplorable ignorance—the lowest point in book learning ever reached in America.[6] Priscilla Alden of Plymouth could not sign her name. Mary Williams, wife of Roger Williams, signed by her mark. In Pennsylvania parents were required, by the provisions of an ordinance passed in 1683, to see that their children could read and write; many elementary schools were established as part of the organization of the churches of the various Protestant sects. In 1671 Governor Berkeley of Virginia praised God that there were no free schools in his colony, but by 1724 twelve free schools, though little more than names, had

---

[5] "Above all, the German is accused of illiteracy. 'God save the mark!' The man whose first care was to erect his church and then establish his parish school in or beside it, illiterate? Is it illiterate when, almost without exception and under the most adverse circumstances, a class of people can not only read and write their own language, but, frequently, that of their neighbor also?" H. M. M. Richards, *German Leaven*, 8. Fiske, *Dutch and Quaker Colonies*, II, 350, says that an interesting feature of the German sects in Pennsylvania was their learning and devotion to literature.

[6] West, *American History and Government*, 161.

been established by endowments of wealthy planters. South of that colony there was no system of schools whatever. With few notable exceptions the only private libraries of consequence were the theological collections of the clergy. In 1700 there was not an American newspaper, the Boston *News Letter* appearing first in 1704.[7]

President C. F. Thwing writes: "Intellectual relationships and motives were in fact lacking in the Plymouth Colony. It was not until the first generation had passed away that public schools were formally established. It is also significant that among the graduates of Harvard College from 1642, when the first degrees were conferred, down to the year 1658, comprising no less than ninety-seven men, are found the names of only one native and two residents of Plymouth Colony."[8]

We are authorized to infer from these citations that intellectual development was on no very high level in any of the colonies, and that the Germans, if they were indeed ignorant, were not exceptions. But no one can read the history of the Pennsylvania Germans without being impressed with the fact that they had an unusually large number of

[7] *Ibid.*
[8] "Pligrim's Motive and Contribution" in *Hibbert Journal*, XIX (Oct. 1920), 78.

exceptionally intelligent and progressive men.
They furnished the State with twelve governors;
they "import many books from Germany," said
Franklin; their physical life was leavened with
much that was intellectual, as appears from the
history of Germantown; they were among the
foremost printers and publishers, founders of industries, casters of type, bookbinders, paper mill
builders and pioneers in many branches of art and
science; and to them goes the credit and distinction of having presented America with the first
great native astronomer, David Rittenhouse, a
genius not of local but of world-wide fame, and
Godfrey, the inventor of the quadrant. The first
serious dramatist of America was a son of Godfrey.[9] They gave us General Peter Mühlenberg;
Frederick Mühlenberg, the first Speaker of the
House of Representatives; the first treasurer
of the United States, Michael Hillegas; the first
Public Printer, Henry Miller; a German manu-
facturer furnished most of the cannon and rifles
for Washington's Army;[10] when Congress was
about to refuse more money for the army,
one man rose and said: "I am only a poor
ginger-bread baker, but write my name down

---

[9] Fiske, *op. cit.*, II, 323, quotes a lengthy passage from one of his
dramas and speaks of his work in terms of high praise. His career was
cut short by early death.
[10] Seibel.

for £200"; his name was Christoph Ludwig, later purveyor for the Revolutionary army; and Margareta Riell for several months provided the American soldiers with bread, refusing to accept payment, and in addition subscribed 1,500 guineas for the American cause; Hillegas came to the aid of the government in the Spring of 1780, as one of several patriots, with his private means to relieve the distress of Washington's soldiers, and in 1781 became one of the founders of the Bank of North America, which afforded liberal support to the government during its financial difficulties.

From the midst of the German pioneers issued many of the pathfinders in the farther West and the first navigators of the Ohio river between Pittsburg and New Orleans. Prominent in the outlying settlements were these Pennsylvania Germans, clearing the forests and building substantial farms. Many lived in the more populous cities. When General Steuben was on his way to join Washington at Valley Forge in 1778, he stopped at Lancaster, then the largest inland town, and was tendered a ball at which all the fashionable people of the day gathered to welcome him. "The baron," says one writer, "was delighted to converse with the German girls in his native tongue." North, his future aide, writes: "His reputation had preceded him, . . . and those who yet remember his graceful entry and manner in a ball-room, . . . can easily conceive the feelings of his countrymen and of their assembled wives and daughters; they might indeed, with honest feeling, have thanked God that they had no reason to be ashamed of him."[11]

The early hardships of these peaceful invaders is a chapter to itself. Thousands indentured themselves to shipmasters and were compelled to work out their passage money; they were indentured servants, "redemptioners," as they were later termed; but they formed a class distinct from the indentured servants that England sent over by thousands, many of them from the slums of London. Their sufferings on shipboard were often frightful. Caspar Wistar wrote in 1732: "Last year a ship was 24 weeks at sea and of the 150 passengers on board thereof more than 100 died of hunger and privations."

If industry was an important factor in the development of the colonies, the Germans assuredly deserve unqualified praise. In the labor that was to be performed they had a lion's share. They stand in the forefront as tillers of the soil and in turning its products to account. Their lot was hard. The primitive roads naturally were inadequate. Indian trails often afforded the only prac-

[11] Kapp. *Steuben*, 104.

ticable paths. People rejoiced if the government cut a road through the woods, cleared the ground to some extent and threw temporary bridges across the creeks and streams. Most of the farmers had no wagons. Some improvised trucks, the wheels of which were blocks cut from a tree trunk, drawn by horses whose harness consisted of untanned skins. During the winter months all communication between the settlements ceased.

The Germans were among the first to introduce the culture of grapes, though their earliest attempts were attended with great difficulties, owing to the heavy forests which absorbed the moisture of the soil, and to the ravages of many pernicious insects which destroyed their plants. On the other hand, they succeeded admirably with their fields and gardens, and with livestock. Not only were the greater varieties of the fruits of the soil introduced by them, but they also set the example in improved methods of soil treatment, fertilization and rotation of crops.

Pennsylvania, as early as the first three decades of the 18th century was able to export rich cargoes of grain to the West Indies and to Spain. The best horses, cattle and sheep came from the German farms.[12]

---

[12] In New York State the Germans along the Hudson and Mohawk were not less distinguished for their fine farms. Two years after their

In 1754 Pownall, late provincial governor of Massachusetts, wrote: "Between Lancaster and Wright's Ferry (on the Susquehanna) I saw some of the finest farms one can conceive, and in the highest state of culture, particularly one that was the estate of a Switzer. Here it was I first saw the method of watering a whole range of pastures and meadows on a hillside by little troughs cut in the side of the hill, along which the water from springs was conducted, so as that when the outlets of these troughs were stopped at the end the water ran over the sides and watered all the ground between that and the other trough next below it. I dare say this method may be in use in England. I never saw it there, but saw it first here."[13]

The French botanist, Michaux, who visited the United States in 1802 under a commission from the French Minister Chaptal, reported "The pre-eminent cultivation of the country and the superior conditions of the hedges and fences which separate their lands from those of their neighbors, sufficiently indicate that these are German settlements. Everything with them evidences that pros-

---

first settlements in Virginia, it has been stated, the Germans were relieved for seven years of all taxation by the Assembly in consideration of their valuable service to the development of agriculture.

[13] *Penn. Mag.*, XVIII, 215.

perity which is the reward of industry and love of work."[14]

They helped to make the plow in the coat-of-arms of the State of Pennsylvania a symbol of respectability, and it was due to this spirit of industry that mills were built at an early date to obtain the most essential staff of life, flour. It is interesting to read the testimony of a German named Ernest Becker. "When I came to Easton,"[15] he writes, "I found only three houses there. My object was to work at my trade, that of baker. But it was not an easy matter. To get flour I had to go to Bethlehem, where a mill had been built some years before, and as there were no roads I had to take my sack and follow an Indian trail, returning in the same way with the bag of flour on my back. Many a time I had to get my supplies in the same way."[16]

Commercially the Germans had to concede the advantage to the English, but in industrial pursuits and in mechanical trades they were pre-eminent, and it is probably not an accident that Pennsylvania, where the Germans were numerically more largely represented than anywhere else, became one of the leading industrial States in the Union. The founders of Germantown en-

[14] Bosse, *Das deutsche Element,* 63.
[15] Probably about 1729.
[16] *Ibid.,* 63.

gaged in the cultivation of flax and the weaving of linen, for which a great demand was soon created in Philadelphia where these commodities were regularly marketed. The first foundry in Lancaster County was started in 1726 by a man named Kurtz.[17] As early as 1749 firearms were manufactured at Strasburg, Lancaster County, by Johann Fondersmith, who was able to maintain his reputation for the quality of his product for over half a century. Proof of this is furnished by Prince Bernard of Weimar, who visited Lancaster in 1826 and published a description of his travels, in which he said: "Lancaster has the reputation of making the best rifles in the United States. I bought one for $11 to take home as a curiosity."[18] During the Revolution, a man named Eberle made "bayonets which are the equal of those of Damascus."[19] Baron Friedrich Wilhelm Stiegel enjoyed a widespread reputation for his iron stoves. He devised the Elizabeth furnace, opened one of the first glass factories in the United States and built an iron foundry at Schaeferstown, Lebanon County, where he produced his famous stoves.[20]

The Germans of this period who left their homes largely because of their religious views and

[17] *Ibid.,* 63.
[18] *Ibid.,* 63.
[19] *Ibid.,* 63.
[20] *Ibid.,* 64.

sentiments were men and women of sound moral
and physical stock, and they contributed not a little
to giving the German element in the colonies a
reputation for diligence and honesty. Their intellectual vision may have been circumscribed; art
and science little known; but they had sound
hearts, and possessed virtues which at that period
were most needed, simple faith, industry and forti-
tude. But they also had poetry and music, especially of a religious character, fostered in the
monastery of Ephrata. Truly humane and Christian, too, was the attitude of the Germans toward
the negroes and Indians. It is indeed at once
touching and exalting to consider how, themselves
beset with poverty, hardships and violence, they
raised their voices seriously and in one accord for
the freedom of the despised negro. The Christian
Germans held slavery incompatible with Christianity, as declared in their ancient code of laws,
the *Sachsenspiegel:* "Common sense and Christianity both teach that no man's body can belong
to another." It was at the insistence of the Germans that the governor of Pennsylvania felt
obliged to submit to the Assembly in 1688 their
demand for permanently suppressing the slave
trade. The petition however was denied, whereupon Germans began to buy slaves whom they
manumitted, and by example as well as by pleading

among their acquaintances they effected substantial modifications of the practice. The Moravians especially were prominent in this direction, in consequence of which they were subjected to many vexations. In Georgia the Salzburgers similarly distinguished themselves. They so vigorously opposed the introduction of slavery that civil conflicts were narrowly averted.

The western border counties of Pennsylvania were constantly exposed to Indian attacks. Here many Germans were settled. Their danger and the neglect of their interests by the provincial assembly were destined to have a strong political influence on future events, as we shall see presently. With Pennsylvania is most intimately connected the name and fame of a regiment that deserves to be commemorated here in brief outlines.

At the outbreak of the French and Indian war (1756-1763), the British government organized the "Royal American" regiment for service in the colonies. It was to consist of four battalions of one thousand men each. Fifty of the officers were to be foreign Protestants, while the enlisted men were to be raised principally from among the German settlers in America. The immediate commander, General Bouquet, was a native of Berne,

Switzerland, in the Dutch service, but became an English colonial officer and a Pennsylvanian by naturalization. Smollet says that Germans and Swiss who composed the regiment, even those born in the colonies, had not learned to speak or understand the English language; but they were strong, hardy men, accustomed to the climate, particularly proper to oppose the French. It was then deemed necessary to appoint some officers who understood military discipline and the German language, and as a sufficient number of such could not be found among the English, it was decided to bring over and grant commissions to a number of German and Swiss officers and engineers. The ranks were filled chiefly from the German immigrants to Pennsylvania and other provinces; and when the Indian war broke out it was chiefly they, though they had now for six years been engaged in the rough and lonely service of the frontier and forests, who like military hermits held the detached posts.of the western border."[21]

Few of the Royal Americans survived the withering storms of the Indian conflict in which they were continuously engaged. "Bouquet's name and fame are alike overlaid with dust. Yet he and his regiment of Germans acted a brave

[21] Parkman, *Conspiracy of Pontiac*, II, 30, 31.

part in their time, and have deserved better of their country than the oblivion which has fallen upon them."[22]   .

[22] Bittinger, *Germans in Colonial Times,* 211.   For a full account of Bouquet's expedition with a much inferior force over the same ground where Braddock had failed, see Parkman, *Conspiracy of Pontiac,* II, ch. xix, xx. Burgess says: "In our Colonial Period almost the entire western border of our country was occupied by Germans.   It fell to them, therefore, to defend, in the first instance, the colonists from the attacks of the French and the Indians.   They formed what was known in those times as the Regiment of Royal Americans, a brigade rather than a regiment, numbering some four thousand men, and the bands led by Nicholas Herkimer and Conrad Weiser. . . . It enabled us to resist successfully the French and their Indian allies in the Seven Years War, which they made upon us from 1756 to 1763, and it gave us a nucleus for our Revolutionary Army." *European War of 1914,* 114.

CHAPTER V

The Germans and the Revolutionary Movement in Pennsylvania—Together with the Irish the Determining Factor in Separation from England—Political Evolution—The Franchise.

THE Americans of the days immediately preceding the Revolution "who were of German birth or descent, formed a large part of the population of the United States; they can not well be reckoned at less than a twelfth of the whole, and perhaps formed even a larger proportion of the insurgent people. At the commencement of the Revolution, we hear little of them, not from their want of zeal in the good cause, but from their modesty. . . . But when the resolution was taken, no part of the country was more determined in its patriotism than the German counties of Pennsylvania and Virginia. Neither they nor their descendants have laid claim to all the praise that was their due."[1]

We are not sure that modesty was the determining motive for their reserved attitude toward

[1] Bancroft, introduction to Kapp's *Steuben*.

independence, as stated by Bancroft. The virgin
soil of America did not favor the transplanting of
medieval political ideals; it nourished a population that had come with nothing but willing hands,
its intelligence and its will-power. While the English very largely betokened devotion to England,
its laws, customs and manners, these were alien
institutions to the German element, and hence it
rallied quickly to the cry of independence.

When the democratic party had control of the
Pennsylvania colonial convention in 1739 it re-
jected the demands of the British government for
men and money for the war with Spain. The
people refused to fight for British aggrandizement
while ready to protect their coasts from the
Spaniards and their ships. A century and a half
of restless endeavor had passed over a country
widely separated from Europe. Time had fitted
for independence those who had embarked to
cross the ocean in search of liberty; had created a
democratic constitution which was related to the
English more in form and tradition than in vital
principles. America had reached the age of dis-
cretion. The Stamp Act and other oppressive
measures impelled the Anglo-American element to
an assertion of independence, though the majority
of them did not in the beginning strive for
absolute separation from the country of their

origin. Eventually the determining factors, as will be shown, as far as Pennsylvania is concerned, were the Irish and the Germans. Numerous as were the Germans, their influence on public affairs in the beginning was limited. All the Crown and colonial officials, as well as a majority of the members of the Pennsylvania Assembly, were men of English birth or descent. The right of voting for members, or being voted for to membership in the Assembly was restricted to native English subjects of the Crown, or to persons naturalized either in England or in the provinces, of twenty-one years of age, who were freeholders in the colony, with fifty acres of land, twelve of them cultivated, or who possessed £50 sterling and had been residents of the province two years. To acquire citizenship was involved with many formalities and for that reason was but little sought by the Germans, though their proverbial apathy was doubtless not a little responsible.

The population of Pennsylvania at this period may be broadly separated into three strata. At the top the Penn proprietors of the province; next the Quakers, in control of the Assembly, then the people generally, mainly the Irish and Germans.[2]

[2] "In no State was there a larger percentage of non-English races and non-English religions than in Pennsylvania. Germans, Dutch, Swedes, Welsh, Scotch and Irish formed a majority of the inhabitants, and none of these elements felt any identity with England. At no time had they

Among all these prevailed a state of latent hostility in the struggle for power and the retention of privileges.   However, not only racial but also geographical considerations and a situation of extreme critical emergency entered into their contentions.   The proprietors, living in England, were represented by a governor, to whom they could issue their orders and prevent the passage of all tax legislation assessing their lands, while at the same time they did not scruple to employ harsh measures to force payments of their rentals, "often at a time when the cultivator was hard pressed to earn a livelihood for his family."

On the other hand, the Quakers stood upon their rights as the first comers and framers of the original compact of government.   Impelled by a sense of ownership in the colony, they were reluctant to admit others to their possession.   They had forced the constitution of 1701 upon Penn, and therefore considered themselves justified in preventing the later immigrants from sharing their power.   Practically in control of the Assembly, supported by a favored element of well-to-do Germans, they were on the one hand at odds with the proprietors and on the other with the mass of

more than a passive spirit of attraction to Great Britain, and nothing could have been more active than the opposition of the Irish or German element when once aroused." Lincoln, *Revolutionary Movement in Pennsylvania*, 141. Cf. also, Greene, *Provincial America*, 234, 235.

the population. "The English," says Lincoln, "were the original holders of power, but only during a few years did they form a majority of the people. By ingenious political management—for the Assembly granted the suffrage to those only . who supported its authority—the English counties retained control of the Assembly until the Revolution, but it was only because of the gross inequality of representation";[3] the policy of the English crown in hindering the naturalization of Germans in America alienated many from British allegiance.[4]

Racial differences, even at that early period,

---

[3] *Revolutionary Movement*, 13.

[4] Baer, *Germans in Pennsylvania*, 11, says, The Germans could acquire citizenship only by naturalization. When English, Scotch or Irish came to the Province, being subjects of Great Britain, they acquired, subject to the Proprietary Law, full rights of citizenship; but the Germans were not British subjects, and special acts were from time to time passed admitting some of the Germans to citizenship. In 1721 many Palatines petitioned for naturalization. After considerable delay the bill passed the Assembly, but it was vetoed by Governor Keith. . . . The difficulties surrounding naturalization prevented the larger number of Germans from becoming British subjects and consequently they could have no vote or voice in the government of the Province. P. 3, "They persistently entreated the Government to pass naturalization laws to enable them to become citizens." Doubtless nativism and race discrimination entered into the matter, and the same contentions arose that Dr. Benjamin Rush brought to the attention of the Legislature as quoted in his *Manners of the German Inhabitants in Pennsylvania*, 1789, in the following exhortation: "Do not contend with their prejudice in favor of their language. It will be the channel through which the knowledge and discoveries of the wisest nations in Europe may be conveyed into our country. . . . Invite them to share in the power and offices of government; it will be the means of producing a union in principle and conduct between them and all those enlightened fellow-citizens who are descended from the other nations." Quoted by Richards, *German Pioneers in Pennsylvania*.

favored the growth of democracy, while all creeds combined to prevent the domination of the English church, and all the diverse elements rallied spontaneously to oppose English political control. Most numerous among the immigrants preceding the Revolution were the Germans, and so large was their influx that, as already pointed out, serious apprehension became manifest during the second quarter of the eighteenth century that they would establish an independent State within the province, in retaliation for the injustice with which they had been treated in legislative enactments. These Germans had no ties of blood with England; and more political sagacity would readily have given them a commanding position;[5] but at no time during the eighteenth century was the Pennsylvania German able to conduct an independent political movement. The capacity for organization which his two rivals, the Quakers and the Irish, seemed to have inherited, was not his. In all the colonial conflicts the Germans appear as the allies—often the valuable allies—of other races,[6] though in time they became an important factor in colonial politics.[7]

Then, as now, the wealthier Germans in the

[5] "Within the province the Germans held the balance of power." Lincoln, *op. cit.*, 37.

[6] *Ibid.*, 26.

[7] Greene, *Provincial America*, 232.

eastern section of the State formed themselves
into a separate class from the poorer; and with
the first stirrings of political unrest they sought
the security of their own interests in disregard of
those of the others. Friction with the proprietors
was increasing, and with the ever-widening breach
between the well-settled eastern part of the province and the Indian border part of the West, the
wealthier Germans in 1775 were admitted into the
social aristocracy that controlled Pennsylvania's
politics. With the accession of these leaders, the
Friends, conceiving it impossible for the western
population to organize an independent movement,
felt confident of keeping the control of the province in their own hands.

In the exposed western border counties, however, the Germans and the Irish had common
interests.[8] They had practically been abandoned
to their fate by the Assembly in their resistance
to Indian depredations and pillage, for the
Quakers regarded the Indians as their wards.[9]
Both prayed for protection from the Indians and
from the colonial land companies that were op-

---

[8] "The Scotch-Irish, like the Germans, were not regarded with unmixed satisfaction. During the early years they received liberal terms
and were encouraged to form barrier settlements on the frontier."
Ibid., 233. "In Pennsylvania the Germans shared with the Scotch and
Irish the distinction of defending the permanent settlements of the mid-
land counties," Faust, I, 267.

[9] See Parkman, *Pontiac.*

pressing them. Both wished increased representation in the colonial Assembly; and, tired of
government interference, they were ready, when
the Revolution came, to cast off the control of
the eastern oligarchy. Their common grievances
found expression in a general movement of political upheaval. Its direction fell to the Irish, who
were more capable leaders, but no people more
eagerly insisted on equal political rights than the
Germans, and no members of the convention that
presently assembled had more radical ideas con-
concerning constitutions than the delegates from
the German districts.[10]

It needed only the sagacious leadership that
fortunately was at hand to swell the movement
into a revolution. The western Germans, equally
hostile toward Great Britain and the old oligarchy, felt no promptings of blood allegiance, and
they held the balance of power. The Irish might
express dislike for England and distrust for British promises; but whether they should succeed or
fail in their efforts was to be determined by their
ability to obtain the support of the Germans and
by their cleverness in overcoming the conservatism
of the east.[11]

Once aroused, the Germans were not behind the

---

[10] Lincoln, *op. cit.*, 26, 27.
[11] *Ibid.*, 36.

Irish in zeal and energy. The German county of Northampton anticipated the radical forces in Philadelphia by holding a meeting on December 21, 1774, to provide for the common defense of the colonies. More than half of the twenty-four members of the County Committee were of German descent, and two-thirds of the Standing Committee that later controlled the county, were Germans, while also the great majority of the county's enrollment was of that race. So fixed was their purpose that, despite the efforts of the wealthy men of the east to control them, even the Germans of Philadelphia abandoned the Quaker cause. The influence of the wealthy Germans had been weakened and the opposition of the poorer strengthened by the offers of the revolutionary leaders of an equal voice in colonial legislation, equality with natives in the American army and the same religious toleration as previously experienced under Quaker supremacy;—"and the race as a whole pronounced for independence of both King and Assembly."[12]

John Dickinson in March, 1774, wrote to Lee that "the people throughout the country look forward to extremes, with revolution. Of these the brave Germans, many of whom have seen service,

[12] *Ibid.*, 27.

are in every sense truly respectable,"[13] and in
June, 1775, a letter from Philadelphia to London
said: "It is amazing to see the spirit of the Germans among us. . . . They speak with infinite
pleasure of sacrificing their lives and property for
the preservation of liberty, which they know full
well how to value, from its deprivation by des-
potick Princes."[14]   Alexander Graydon's testimony in his memoirs is to the same effect and the
press tells no different story.[15]

The gauge of battle had been thrown down, and
the Germans were enlisted in the cause of liberty
to their full bent.   Quakers and Episcopalians
were not averse to a change from proprietary government to the status of a crown colony, but both
were opposed to independence such as was demanded by the democratic German-Irish party,
with its hostility to State Church and indifference
to English traditions and policies.

The delegates from Pennsylvania to the Continental Congress, chosen November 4, 1775, were
John Dickinson, Robert Morris, Benjamin Franklin, Charles Humphreys, Edward Biddle, Thomas
Willing, Andrew Allen and James Wilson, the
very flower of the moneyed and intellectual aristocracy of the Province.

[13] Force, Am. Archives, 4th ser. I, 726.
[14] Ibid., II, 1,034.
[15] Lincoln, op. cit., 32, n.

On November 9, 1775, the Assembly gave these delegates instructions in regard to the policy they were to pursue in Congress as the representatives of Pennsylvania. They were told: "You should use your utmost endeavors to agree upon and recommend all such measures as you shall judge to afford the best prospects of obtaining the redress of American grievances, but utterly reject any proposition (should such be made) that may cause or lead to a separation from the mother country or a change in the form of this government" (the Charter Government of the province).

Seeing in this resolution that Pennsylvania was not inclined to fall in with the policy of complete independence, Congress resolved "that it be recommended to the different Colonies where no government sufficient to the exigencies of their affairs has been established, to establish such a government as would answer the purpose."

Thus encouraged, the democratic party of Pennsylvania, calling themselves Whigs, insisted that the Penn Charter did not give them a government "suited to the exigencies of their affairs" and declared that it should be abolished in order that a popular convention might frame a new one. The majority of the Assembly denied both propositions, but on June 8, 1776, after a heated discussion, rescinded its instructions to the delegates adopted November 9 of the year before, and authorized them by new instructions to concur with other delegates in Congress in forming contracts with "the united Colonies, including treaties with foreign kingdoms and such measures as they should judge necessary for promoting the liberty, etc., of the people of the Province, reserving to said people the sole and exclusive right of regulating the internal government of the same."

This resolution never came to a vote, for when on June 14 it was to be put upon its passage the necessary two-thirds majority was not at hand. The Whigs having by a secret understanding withdrawn, never returned to their seats, and the Assembly as a result of this desertion continued to lead a shadowy existence without being able to muster a quorum until it passed out of existence in August, 1776.

There was now no restraining the popular movement. The Assembly being ignored and treated as non-existent, a group of ardent democrats in Philadelphia decided to call a convention and issued summonses to the several counties of the province to send delegates to meet in Philadelphia on June 18 for the purpose of organizing a government of the people. In order to obtain a majority it was necessary to have representatives present irrespective of their right to vote under the English laws.

The Germans were irretrievably lost to the Quaker cause, but the election in May, 1776, was carried by the Conservatives through the suppression, it was claimed, of the German vote. The general conference of the committees took place at Carpenter's Hall, with 108 delegates present; few if any of the Assembly appeared. On the 19th unanimous approval was given to the action of Congress respecting the formation of States, and on the same day the German militia of Philadelphia presented a petition praying that all taxable Associators be given the right to vote for members of the convention and a share in the government of the State. The petition was favorably received. It afforded the conference an opportunity to gain the support of a large faction that had long been denied its rights and that smarted under the injustice of having withheld from it the franchise and a voice in the provincial government. On June 20 a resolution was adopted giving the franchise to every Associator 21 years of age, who had resided one year in the colony and been assessed for provincial or county taxes. The existing government of the colony was condemned as incompetent and it was recommended that a new one be founded by authority of the people. With equal unanimity the delegates, on the 24th, declared for themselves and their constituents their willingness to concur in a Congressional declaration of independence.

At least one-fifth of the delegates from Philadelphia were Germans, while many others, declared Christopher Marshall, were working hard to get the army into proper condition. On September 28, 1776, a State constitution was adopted. The action of the Philadelphia convention was decisive and destined to have far-reaching effect on the future history of the country. The Assembly of Pennsylvania had struggled long and bitterly with the problem that was agitating the people. It had made one concession after another. In October, 1775, it had subscribed to the usual form of allegiance to the King; under pressure it abolished the oath. This not having satisfied the patriots, the committee of inspection of Philadelphia had addressed a memorial to Congress representing that the Assembly had forfeited the confidence of the people, that it did not truly represent the sentiment of the province, and that steps had been taken for calling a popular convention.

In Congress the situation with regard to the pending Declaration of Independence was critical. "There could be no independence while

Pennsylvania did not consent," writes Charles J. Stille, "and there seemed at that time little prospect that she would agree to a separation of any kind while her policy was controlled by her legal Assembly."[16]

Benjamin Franklin was the only delegate in Congress from Pennsylvania chosen in November, 1775, who voted for and signed the Declaration of Independence voluntarily. Of that delegation when the vote was taken on the second of July, Dickinson and Morris were absent, Wilson was much opposed to it, but appended his signature, and Willing and Humphreys voted against it. But though divided against themselves within the delegation, the assenting action of those who did sign "the death warrant of royal power on this continent" crowned Pennsylvania the Keystone State—the keystone in the arch of liberty.

For the first time the Germans had exerted a mass influence in American political life, and by turning the scale against the Assembly which had persistently abandoned them to the horrors of Indian depredations and tortures, they had proved a deciding factor in the bringing of vital support to the champions of national independence.[17] And

[16] "Pennsylvania and the Declaration of Independence," *Penn. Mag. of History and Biography,* 1889, No. 4.
[17] "Had it not been for the Pennsylvania Germans there would have been no Declaration of Independence on July 4, 1776, and today the

now that the die had been cast they forthrightly faced the consequences and, as Lincoln testifies, "a careful study of the time will show that it was in no half-hearted manner that the Germans took up the cause of colonial and continental liberty."[18]

great United States, each an empire in itself, might still be comparatively feeble colonies of Great Britain." Richards, *The German Leaven in the Pennsylvania Loaf.* "At the various conventions held in Philadelphia from 1775 on, a large proportion of delegates from Berks, Lancaster, York, Northampton and other counties were Germans. We may take as a single example the Convention of 1776, of which Franklin was president. Out of 96 delegates 22 were Germans; four of the eight sent by Lancaster and three of the eight sent by Berks were Germans. Northampton sent six. Among them were Mühlenberg, Hillegas, Slagle, Hubley, Kuhn, Arndt, Levan, Hiestand, etc.," Kuhns, *German and Swiss Settlements,* 208.

[18] *Revolutionary Movement in Pennsylvania,* 31.

CHAPTER VI

The Germans in the Revolution—The Advance Guard — Prominent Soldiers — Von Steuben, Mühlenberg, Herkimer — The Battle of Oriskany and its Bearings on the Result.

FAUST gives what he regards as a conservative estimate of the number of Germans in the colonies at the outbreak of the Revolutionary war. His figures are based upon church censuses, documentary evidence and contemporary computations, and reach the total of 225,000, divided as follows:

New England	1,500
New York	25,000
Pennsylvania	110,000
New Jersey	15,000
Maryland-Delaware	20,500
Virginia-West Virginia ...	25,000
North Carolina	8,000
South Carolina	15,000
Georgia	5,000
	225,000

The majority of these dwelt along the frontiers and comprised a rugged element. They formed not only a valuable integral factor of the patriot army as raw material by reason of their numbers, but many of them had previously served against the French and Indians, from Ticonderoga to Quebec, as well as against Pontiac. They now marched out as free men to prove their patriotism and with eagerness to help in expelling the last European governor ruling over an American colony.

The events at Lexington and Concord stirred to its depths the patriotic spirit that had been aroused in the German element everywhere. The first blow had been struck. None more keenly felt the value of the precious bestowal of liberty under the newly-proclaimed order. Again and again they had been called upon to defend their cabins from midnight attacks; many of their relatives had perished under the tomahawk and scalping knife, and the freedom of the woods and valleys attuned their hearts to the sound of political independence. They had grown with their allotted spaces. The British were besieged within the confines of Boston; Washington had just been commissioned commander-in-chief, "and on June 14, 1775, the Continental Congress had issued a call for troops to form his army. Hardly had a month elapsed, barely time enough for the call to be received and the recruits gathered, when there

marched into the American camp a body of
hunters, few less than six feet in height, clad in
white hunting shirts and leggins, and carrying before them a green standard, in the center of which
was a crimson square bearing the device of a
panther . . . attempting the pass defended by a
hunter, clad in white, and armed with a spear, be-
neath all the motto, 'Domari Nolo'. It was
the advance guard of the grand Continental
Army, the Pennsylvania Riflemen, nearly one-
half of whom were Pennsylvania Germans, and
one-third of whose companies were commanded by
men of the same race. Of these troops, Captain
Nagel's company of Berks County 'Dutchmen'
arrived from Reading in advance on July 18,
1775, the first defenders of the Revolution."[1]

The first announcement of the adoption of the
Declaration of Independence was printed in the
Philadelphia *Staatsbote*.[2] Everywhere the call to

[1] Richards, *German Leaven*, 15.
[2] "We read in the yellowed files of Miller's *Staatsbote* . . . set forth
in the boldest antique type that the office could boast: 'Philadelphia, den
5 Juli Gestern hat der achtbare Congress dieses vesten Landes die
vereinigten Colonien freye und unabhängige Staaten erkläret. Die
Declaration in English ist gesetzt in der Presse; sie ist datirt den 4ten
Juli, 1776, und wird heut oder morgen in druck erscheinen.'
"As the *Staatsbote* was the only Philadelphia paper which appeared
on Friday, and the Declaration was adopted on Thursday, it was thus
through the columns of a Pennsylvania-German paper that the first
news of the independence was published." Bittinger, *Germans in Colonial
Times*, 241. The author has not been able to confirm the statement of
various writers that the full text of the Declaration was first printed in
Christoph Sauer's Germantown *Hochdeutsch-Pennsylvanische Geschichts-
schreiber*.

arms exercised an electrical effect upon the German population. Squads of German riflemen tramped 600 miles from Virginia to Massachusetts. Instead of the six companies called for, Pennsylvania sent nine, four of them entirely German.[3] The Mennonites, Dunkards and Moravians were religiously opposed to taking up arms. Many of them fled westward into new regions of forest and wilderness to escape persecution, but those who remained, though refusing to fight, bravely performed their duty of supplying the army with cattle and grain; and a considerable number, together with numerous Quakers, presently put aside their religious scruples and armed themselves for the fray.

One of the most influential agents in fanning the flames of revolution was the *Staatsbote,* mentioned above, published by Henry Miller, afterwards the official printer of Congress. It was read in sections as remote as the Valley of Virginia. The issue of March 19, 1776, contains an appeal to the Germans, beginning: "Remember that your forefathers emigrated to America to escape bondage and to enjoy liberty."[4]

In 1775, says Rosengarten, the vestries of the German Lutheran and Reformed churches at

---

[3] Seibel, *Hyphen in American History.* See Seidensticker, *Geschichtsbilder,* "Die Deutschen im Revolutions-Kriege."
[4] *Virginia Magazine,* X, 45.

Philadelphia sent a pamphlet of forty pages to the
Germans of New York and North Carolina, stat-
ing that their brethren in the near and remote
parts of Pennsylvania had distinguished themselves by forming not only a militia but a select
corps of sharpshooters, ready to march whenever
required, while those who could not perform military service were willing to contribute according
to their ability.[5] They urged the Germans of
other colonies to give their support to the common
cause, to carry out the measures of Congress, and
to rise in arms against the oppression and des-
potism of the British government. The volunteers
of Pennsylvania were called "Associators," and
the Germans among them had their headquarters
in the Lutheran schoolhouse in Philadelphia.

[5] "I have seen it stated in an old document of the time (I forget the
writer), that if it were· not for the Pennsylvania Dutch women the
army could not keep the field a month."—Sachse, *True Heroes of
Provincial Pennsylvania.* Rittenhouse, scientist and philosopher though
he was, given to sedentary pursuits, took an active part in the cause of
patriotism as an official of the Council of Safety. Wilson, *American
People,* II, 259, prints the following:

"In Council of Safety
"Philadelphia, December 8, 1776.

"*Sir,* There is certain intelligence of General Howe's army being
yesterday on its march from Brunswick to Princeton, which puts it
beyond a doubt that he intends for this city—This glorious opportunity
for signalizing himself in defence of our country, and securing the
Rights of America forever, will be seized by every man who has a
spark of patriotic fire in his bosom. We entreat you to march the
Militia under your command with all possible expedition to this city, and
bring with you as many waggons as you can possibly procure, which you
are hereby authorized to impress, if they cannot be had otherwise—
Delay not a moment, it may be fatal and subject you and all you hold

In the Valley of the Blue Ridge, relates Bancroft, the German congregations, quickened by the preaching of Mühlenberg, were eager to take up arms.[6]   But long before the final appeal to arms had been sounded, the Germans in the Valley of Virginia had adopted on June 16, 1774, resolutions "that we will pay due submission to such acts of government as His Majesty has a right by law to exercise over his subjects, and to such only."[7]

One of the boldest and earliest declarations was made in New York by the Tryon County Committee of Safety.   The declaration, dated August 27, 1774, sets forth "that we think it is our undeniable Privilege to be taxed only with our own Consent given by ourselves (or by our Representative).   That Taxes otherwise laid and exacted are unjust and unconstitutional.   That the Late Acts of Parliament declarative of their rights of laying internal Taxes on the American Colonies

most dear to the ruffian hands of the enemy, whose cruelties are without distinction and unequalled.

"By Order of the Council,
"David Rittenhouse, Vice-President.

"To the Colonels or Commanding Officers
of the respective Battalions of this State.

"TWO O'CLOCK, P. M.

"The enemy are at Trenton, and all the City Militia are marched to meet them."

[6] *United States*, final ed., V, 147.

[7] Faust, I, 292.

are obvious Incroachments in the Rights and Liberties of the British subjects in America."

In hardly any other connection has nativistic prejudice gone to such lengths in the attempt to minimize and even to ignore the great share of the Germans in the cause of American liberty as in dealing with this famous committee, while on the other hand its history has become so involved with inaccuracies of the other extreme that it is worth a little space here to state the facts as they appear in *The Minute Book of the Committee of Safety of Tryon County, the Old New York Frontier,* reprinted in 1905 by J. Howard Hanson, with notes by Samuel Ludlow Frey.   William L. Stone, in his *Life of Joseph Brant-Thayandenegea* (1838), may err in describing the resolutions of August 27, 1774, as an unqualified declaration of independence antedating that of Congress, but his judgment is decidedly more on the side of justice than statements made about the time that the Oriskany monument was dedicated (1884), when one of the speakers felt obliged to reject most energetically the claim of those who wished to obscure the deeds of the brave Palatine settlers. It is charged against Campbell, the New York historian, by a correspondent of the author, with having "practically retained a whole basketful of documents—never recovered afterwards—bearing on the history of the Germans in the Mohawk Valley, which the owner had entrusted to him."

There is some significance in the fact that the first meeting of the Tryon County Committee of Safety at which the declaration of August 27, 1774, was adopted, was held at the house of Adam Loucks, "one of the Palatines." He was a Justice of the Peace and a man of prominence.

At the second meeting "the resolutions were read and unanimously approved" and the following persons appointed "a standing committee of this district" to correspond with the committees of this and the committees of other counties: Christopher P. Yates, John Frey, Isaac Paris, Andrew Finck, Jr., Andrew Reber, Peter Waggoner, Daniel McDougall, Jacob Clock, George Elker, Jr., Hermanus V. Slyck, Christopher W. Fox, and Anthony V. Vechten. With the exception of two, all were Germans or Dutch. The third meeting, that of May 19, 1775, directed a letter to the Committee of Albany, declaring "we shall not be able to send down any Deputies to the Provincial Congress, as we cannot obtain the Sense of the County soon enough to make it worth our while to send any, but be assured we are not the less attached to American Liberty, for we are determined, though few in number, to let the world see, who are, and who are not Such." Those present were Yates, Frey, Paris, Finck, Reber, Elker, Van Slyck, Fox, and Van Veghten. The fifth clause of the resolution adopted at the fourth meeting, held at the house of Philip W. Fox, May 21, 1775, reads: "That as we abhor a State of Slavery, We do join and unite together under all the ties of Religion, Honor, Justice and Love for our Country, never to become Slaves, and to defend our Freedom with our Lives and Fortunes." Present were, Yates, Paris, Reber, Van Slyck, Fox, McDougall, Finck, Waggoner, and Clock. The members of the Committee living in Cherry Valley were Scotch-Presbyterians, very strict in their ideas of religious observances, and they wrote a vigorous letter protesting against holding meetings on the Sabbath, this resolution having been adopted on Sunday.

In November, 1775, the Committee seems to have consisted of 38 members, as the minutes of the 29th meeting give the names of those present as well as those of "the absentees." Including Herkimer, chairman, who was "absent for sickness," twenty-five were undoubtedly Germans, eight British, three Dutch and two of uncertain origin. The notes attached to the reprint of the *Minute Book* give the history and nativity of most of the members of the Committee, and their author finds that "in fact this phonetic and careless way of spelling family names is confusing and misleading in studying the history of the time." Kapp has done a great deal to clarify the difficulty by correcting errors in the spelling of the names, due partly to ignorance, indifference and partly to clerical faults. The present author finds many such corruptions as Waggoner for Wagner, Fox for Fuchs, Clock for Klock, Petry for Petrie, Visgor for Visscher or Fischer, and Herkimer for Herkheimer, as it appears in the minutes of meetings at which John Eisenlord, himself a German, acted as clerk. He also finds that, first and last, about sixty names appear in the reports of the meetings, and of these forty are German or Dutch (five of the latter), as follows: John Frey, Andrew Finck Jr., Andrew Reber, Peter Waggoner, Jacob Clock, Nicholas and George Herkimer, Seeber, Edward Wall, William Petry, J. Weaver (John Jacob Weber), M. Petry, John Petry, George Wents, J. Franck, Frederick Fox, Christian W. Fox, Augustus Hess, M. Ittig, Frederic Ahrendorf, Adam Fonda, Frederick Visscher or Fisher (probably of Dutch descent), Frederick Hallmer, Hellmer or Halmer, J. and Conrad Pickert, John Eisenlord, Rudolf Shoemaker, Joost Herkimer, Jr., John Kayser, Jr., Henrich Harter or Herter, Henry Heintz, John Demuth or Demoth, Adam Loucks, John J. Clock, Lawrence Zimmerman, Hermanus V. Slyck, A. V. Fechten or Van Vechten, Valkert Vedder or Fedder, Abraham Van Horn; Christian P. Yates, Isaac Paris Daniel McDougall, Cox, J. Moore, Duncan McDougall, Sampson Sammons, Marlatt, Abraham Yates, Samuel Campbell, Samuel Clyde, Thomas Henry, J. Bliven, William Schuyler, James McMaster, Daniel Lane, John Thompson, Christian Nellis or Nelles.

Kapp interprets the large representation of Germans as "proof that the movement rested principally upon the German settlers, as otherwise the majority of the delegates would not have been of that race, and I base my conjecture on the reluctance of the Palatines to take part in public affairs and their aversion to notoriety. It is more than probable that the men with English names acted also as delegates of German constituencies. From East to West the Germans became increasingly numerous. In the Mohawk district the proportion was only two to eight of the delegates; in the Canajoharie, which sent Nicholas Herkheimer and William Siebert (Seeber), the proportion was eight to two; from the Palatine district seven of the eleven were Germans—Johann Frey, Andreas Fink, Andreas Reiber, Peter Wagner, Jakob Klock, George Ecker, and Christian W. Fuchs; in the German Flatts and Kingsland districts only two of the twelve delegates were not German. They are Eduard Wall, Wilhelm Petrie, Johann Petrie, August Hess, Frederich Orendorf, George Wentz, Michel Illig, Friedrich Fuchs, George Herkheimer, Friedrich Helmer and Johann Fink."

.   .   .   .   .   .

On Steuben's services to the American cause as Inspector General and drillmaster of the American army it is not necessary to dwell, save to quote an extract from the "creed" adopted by the officers of the Revolutionary Army at Verplanck's Point in 1782: "We believe that Baron Steuben has made us soldiers, and that he is capable of forming the whole world into a solid column, and displaying it from the center. We believe in his Blue Book. We believe in General Knox and his artillery. And we believe in our bayonets. Amen."[a]

The last sentence but one has more significance than appears on the surface. The majority of the Continental army had no better use for the bayonet than to utilize it as a spit to roast and toast their venison and beefsteak over their camp-fires, and it was only with great difficulty that Steuben could persuade them to employ it as a weapon of offense and defense. Nor did he succeed in making the bayonet popular until after the storming of Stony Point. That battle was won

[a] Quoted on the authority of a magazine clipping.

with the bayonet and gloriously vindicated Steuben's partiality to its use. Few historians have thought it worth while to relate that Steuben received Cornwallis's overtures for surrender at Yorktown, an incident leading to a slight misunderstanding between Steuben and Lafayette. It is here reported on the authority of Kapp.* The deeds of General Mühlenberg and De Kalb need not engage us, as their share in the Revolution should be found in every impartial American history book.

Pennsylvania German-American war annals are replete with the names of self-sacrificing patriots.

* *Steuben,* 228, 458.
"Opinions may differ as to the relative standing of these associates, but there can be little doubt as to the two most closely allied to Washington in that memorable conflict whose skirmishes, as Napoleon has justly observed, changed the entire history of the world. These two were Alexander Hamilton, whose great achievements toward laying the foundations of this Government we are just now beginning to appreciate, and the subject of this biography.

'This later statement may surprise some who have regarded Steuben simply as a drillmaster, but is sustained by a close study of the facts. From the time he joined the famishing army at Valley Forge until he received the overtures for the surrender of Cornwallis at Yorktown, he was at Washington's right hand, planning campaigns, looking after the troops, bringing order out of chaos, turning defeat into victory and on more than one occasion averting what threatened to be a fatal disaster." Doyle, *Steuben.*

See Fiske, *American Revolution,* II, ch. x. When General Charles Lee, in pursuance of his evil design to betray Washington and the colonial cause, ordered the Americans at the Battle of Monmouth to retreat in the moment of victory, Washington rode up and furiously rebuked Lee for his inexplicable conduct. "It was now that the admirable results of Steuben's teachings were to be seen," writes Fiske, p. 64. "The retreating soldiers immediately wheeled and formed under fire with as much coolness and precision as they could have shown on parade, and while they stopped the enemy's progress, Washington rode back and brought up the main body of the army."

There the Hiester Brothers were especially prominent, notably Joseph; John and Daniel were commissioned major and colonel, respectively, and were breveted generals after the war. Each was elected to Congress,—Joseph Hiester for fourteen years,—and he was later elected governor. Among the Germans of the South, Major Elbert, afterwards General Elbert, distinguished himself at Fort Howe, when with 300 men in boats he proceeded to Frederica and captured several British vessels under the walls of the English fortress. Another active German was Col. Mahem of St. Stephan Parish, South Carolina, who fought in Marion's brigade. Such was his fame that the English offered him the command of a regiment. He replied: "A German does not desert his colors!"[10]

In the West, Captain Leonhardt Helm won renown. When Hamilton in 1778 with his British troops moved against Vincennes, the American garrison of the fort consisted of Helm and one private.[11] But Helm took his position by a can-

[10] Von Bosse, *Das deutsche Element*, 84. There were Germans in Anthony Wayne's command. Wm. H. Egle, one time librarian of the Pennsylvania Historical society, wrote Stillé: "With the exception of the Scotch-Irish, who formed about two-thirds of his force, the remainder were almost wholly of German parentage." Stillé, *Anthony Wayne*, 249.

[11] "Poor Helm was promptly deserted by all the creole militia. The latter had been loud in their boasts until the enemy came in view, but as soon as they caught sight of the red-coats they began to slip away and run up to the British to surrender their arms. He was finally left with only one or two men, Americans." Roosevelt, *Winning of the West*, II, 63.

non with burning fuse and demanded to know
what conditions would be granted the garrison if
it surrendered the fort.   Hamilton promised the
usual honors of war, and was not a little chagrined
when he found that the garrison consisted of but
two men.

Other outstanding characters deserve mention:
General George Weedon (Gerhard von Wieden),
who, after serving with Bouquet in Flanders and
in the French and Indian War, settled at Fredericksburg, Va., where John F. D. Smyth describes
him as keeping a public house or inn, and "now
a general officer in the American army, and was
then very active and zealous in blowing the flames
of sedition."[12]   At the outbreak of the Revolution
he became lieutenant-colonel and colonel' of the
Third Virginia Continental, and in 1777 brigadier
general, taking a leading part in the battles of
Brandywine and Germantown, later re-entering
the army under Mühlenberg and commanding the
Virginia militia before Gloucester Point at the
siege of Yorktown.[13]

General Weissenfels was an officer in the British army in New York, but immediately on the outbreak of the war offered his services to Washington.   Having served in the French and Indian

[12] A Tour in the United States, II, 151.
[13] Faust, op. cit., I, 330; Heitman, Historical Register, 579.

War and mounted the Heights of Abraham with the brave Wolfe, to see him "fall in the arms of victory," he served with General Montgomery in the attack on Quebec; as lieutenant-colonel in command of the Third Battalion in the Second New York, inflicting severe losses on the enemy at White Plains; accompanied Washington across the Hudson, took part in the battles of Trenton and Princeton, and was present with his regiment at the capture of Burgoyne. Weissenfels was distinguished for personal gallantry, and was honored by Washington and Congress with marks of grateful acknowledgment.

Heinrich Emanuel Lutterloh was appointed Commissary of forage and foragemaster-general.[14]

An officer whose adventures possess a distinct romantic interest was Joseph Paul Schott, who, like Lutterloh, had been in the service of Frederick the Great and attached to the Duke of Brunswick. Although he had come to serve the British, he soon changed his mind, and seeing the lack of guns and ammunition of the Americans, he decided upon a daring plan to furnish them with this indispensable equipment. His ample means enabled him to sail in the summer of 1776 to the Dutch island of St. Eustache where the Hollanders had established a depot to supply blockade runners.

14 Faust, *op. cit.*, I, 332, says he was quartermaster general.

Schott hired a schooner, loaded it with guns and ammunition at his own expense, and steered for the coast of Virginia. At the mouth of the Chesapeake he found the English fleet blockading the entrance to Hampton Roads. Schott hoisted the British flag, and having dressed his sailors in British uniforms, succeeded in crossing the line before the blockading ships detected his ruse. A broadside did little or no damage and the schooner reached its destination, but was here mistaken for an English vessel. Schott, finding himself fired upon, now raised the white flag and the schooner then anchored in the harbor of Norfolk amid great rejoicing.

His petition for a commission was granted, and at the battle of White Plains, where the Americans owed the withdrawal of their baggage to their excellent batteries, Schott commanded the Third Battery in Knox's artillery. He was sent by Washington into the Pennsylvania districts when the American commander most keenly felt the scarcity of men, and recruited an independent troop of dragoons with permission to appoint his own officers and give commands in German. He was severely wounded and taken prisoner in covering the retreat at the battle of Short Hills, and was offered an English command, which he refused. In 1779 he was exchanged and commanded the right wing in the brigade of General Hand under General Sullivan. The Indians were attacked at Newton (near the present Elmira, N. Y.), their forces annihilated and their villages destroyed.

A dashing Revolutionary soldier and fighter was David Ziegler, who enjoyed the unique distinction of holding the position of commander-in-chief of the American army for a short period. Ziegler was born near Heidelberg in 1748, served in the Russian army under Catherine II, took part in the Turkish-Russian campaign, which ended in the capture of the Crimea in 1774, and came to America the same year, settling in Lancaster, Pa. He joined General William Thompson's battalion, which appeared before Boston, August 2, 1775, largely composed of Pennsylvania Germans, and the second regiment to enroll for the war; served throughout the war, being repeatedly mentioned for distinguished service, and was appointed by General St. Clair Commissioner-General for the Department of Pennsylvania. Major Denny in his diary, refers to him in these words: "As a disciplinarian he has no superior in the whole army."

Ziegler enlisted for the Indian war in the west and served as captain in the only regiment of regulars under General Harmar; built Fort Finney at the mouth of the Big Miami, took part in General Clark's expedition against the Kickapoos on the Wabash, and in 1790 in General Harmar's disastrous expedition on the upper Miami. He distinguished himself in the battle of the Maumee for personal bravery, and, dispatched by General St. Clair with two companies to succor the distressed settlers in and around Marietta, he gained such decisive advantage over the hordes of Indians, and so quickly restored order, that he was hailed as the most popular soldier in the Northwest. In St. Clair's bloody and disastrous campaign, in which he commanded a battalion of regulars, he covered the headlong retreat, and by ceaseless vigilance and strict discipline succeeded, in the face of furious attacks by the Indians, drunk with victory, in leading the scattered American forces back to Fort Washington (Cincinnati). His dash and efficiency had caused his advancement to major in the regular army, and when St. Clair was summoned to Philadelphia to defend his conduct, he invested Ziegler with the temporary authority of commander-in-chief, a position which he held for six weeks. Having resigned his commission, he was elected the first mayor of the recently incorporated city of Cincinnati in 1802 and subsequently re-elected by a large majority in recognition of his services in protecting the settle-

ments in 1791 and 1792, as well as in vindication
of his unjust treatment by the government.[15]
Ziegler died in Cincinnati, September 24, 1811,
sincerely mourned by his fellow citizens.

. . . . . .

We shall here describe an event that was destined to have far-reaching bearings on the history
of American independence.

The Battle of Oriskany has been called the most
savage engagement of the Revolution.   Under
ordinary circumstances it would have been called
a mere skirmish, this "without exception the
bloodiest single conflict in the war of the Revolution. . . . Nothing more horrible than the car-
nage of that battle has ever occurred in the history
of warfare," to quote Elson.[16]   But in its ultimate
bearings it proved one of the most important
events of the Revolution.

Col. St. Leger, commanding a British force, had
landed at Oswego, coming from Canada under
orders to march through the Mohawk Valley to
Albany, there to join Burgoyne, who was coming
down from Canada with a large force by way of
Lake Champlain.   These united forces were to
move down the Hudson River to join Sir Henry
Clinton from New York, to isolate New England
and to cut off all communication between the

[15] *Ibid.,* 409-411.
[16] *United States,* 270, 271.

northern colonies and those of the Center and South. An irresistible force would be concentrated so as to crush all further opposition in New England, and this done it was believed that the other colonies would speedily submit. The Americans had no troops in the field that seemed able to baffle these movements. "Without question, the plan was ably formed; and had the success of the execution been equal to the ingenuity of the design, the reconquest and submission of the thirteen United States must in all probability have followed, and the independence which they proclaimed in 1776 would have been extinguished before it existed a second year. . . . America, if defeated in 1777, would have been suffered to fall unaided."[17]

In the summer of that year occurred events that defeated the well-planned British operations. One of these was the battle of Oriskany. Col. Peter Gansevoort was appointed to command Fort Schuyler, formerly called Fort Stanwix, and held that post in the summer of 1777 when Burgoyne was making his victorious march toward Albany by way of Lake Champlain. The people of the Mohawk Valley were thrown upon their own feeble resources for defense. St. Leger and his Rangers, with Johnson, Butler and Brant (the

[17] Creasy. Morris, *Half Hours with American History*, II, 62.

Indian leader), numbering 1,700, on August 1, 1777, prepared to invest Fort Schuyler, whose garrison consisted of 750 men. General Herkimer was advancing to the aid of the garrison with a force of 800 militia, recruited chiefly from the Palatine settlers in the Mohawk Valley. The brigade was divided into four battalions, the first (Canajoharie) commanded by himself; the second (Palatine District) by Jacob Klock; the third (Mohawk) by Friedrich Fischer, and the fourth (German Flatts and Kingsland) by Hanjost Herkimer. St. Leger had intelligence of the advance of Herkimer and detached a division of Johnson's Greens under Major Watts, Col. Butler with his Rangers and Brant with a strong body of Indians, to intercept him. It is not necessary to go into the details of the battle, in which each side lost a third of its numbers. The Americans remained masters of the field, but Herkimer had received his death-wound.

St. Leger's Indians were disheartened by the large number of their men slain, and when General Arnold sent a messenger among them who reported the advance of a large number of Americans, they deserted and communicated a panic to the rest of the camp, and in a few hours the beleaguering army around Fort Schuyler was flying in terror toward its boats on Oneida Lake. The

Indians, it was said, made merry at the precipitate flight of the English, who threw away their arms and knapsacks, so that nothing would impede their progress.[18]

St. Leger's failure and Baum's defeat at Bennington rendered Burgoyne's position critical. With no help in sight from General Howe or Clinton, and now greatly outnumbered, the British general fought three hopeless battles on September 19, October 7 and 17, and surrendered. Creasy and other authorities regard the Battle of Saratoga as the turning point of the war. France at once consented to a treaty of alliance, which had been long delayed and the negotiations toward which had been almost broken off by the preceding tidings of the victorious march of Burgoyne toward Albany.[19] The first vital blow against the consummation of the British campaign had fallen at Oriskany.

In 1758, at the age of thirty, Herkimer was appointed a lieutenant in the army sent to fight the Indians. He erected a fort that was named in his honor, which he defended with his Palatines for eight months against the joint attacks of the Indians and French. After the French-Indian war he retired to his farm at Canajoharie. At

[18] Lossing.
[19] *Ibid.*, 73.

the outbreak of the Revolutionary war his fame
was so well established that he was named chairman of the Committee of Safety and appointed
brigadier general. Washington entertained the
highest respect and admiration for the veteran.
"He it was," were his words, "who first reversed
the gloomy scene of the Northern campaign. The
hero of the Mohawk Valley served from love of
country, not for reward. He did not want a
Continental command, or money."[20]

. . . .

We are justified in inferring from several circumstances that the Germans occupied a warm
place in the regard of the commander-in-chief and
first President of the United States. In a letter
written by him two years before the Declaration of
Independence, he expresses his desire to settle
some lands in Ohio "by falling on no better
expedient to settle my land with industrious people, than by such an importation," meaning Palatine "redemptioners". We may also judge from
his very cordial relations with Steuben, who was
one of his immediate entourage on taking the oath
of office at his first inauguration and to whom was
addressed his last letter—a strong letter of appreciation and devotion—before the hour set for his
retirement from command of the army.

[20] Lester's *United States*, I, 358.

When Washington's first body-guard was suspected of treasonable sentiments and plans, it was dismissed; and a new body-guard, consisting almost entirely of Germans, was formed. This new body-guard was supported by a troop of cavalry consisting of Germans. This troop stood by Washington during the entire war, and twelve of them escorted him to Mt. Vernon when he retired.[21] In reply to congratulations by the Germans of Philadelphia on his first election, he closed a lengthy letter of appreciation with the words: "From the excellent character for diligence, sobriety and virtue which the Germans in general, who are settled in America have ever maintained, I cannot forbear felicitating myself on receiving from so respectable a number of them such strong assurance of their affection for my person, confidence in my integrity, and real zeal to support me in my endeavors for promoting the welfare of our common country."[22] In the report of the first inaugural parade, "the German Grenadiers under Capt. Scrila" occupy a conspicuous place.[23] On the death of Washington both Houses of Congress adopted a resolution "that there be a funeral procession from congress hall to the Ger-

[21] Burgess, *European War of 1914*, 115.
[22] *Archives of Zion Church*, Philadelphia.
[23] *Gazette of the United States*, May 2, 1789, reprinted in the Philadelphia Bulletin, February 22, 1922.

man Lutheran church . . . and that an oration
be prepared at the request of congress, to be delivered before both houses on that day; . . . The
funeral procession was grand and solemn, and
the eloquent oration which was delivered [in the
German church] by general [Light Horse Harry]
Lee, was heard with profound attention and with
deep interest."[24]

Washington attached great importance to the
treaty with Prussia, for in a letter to Rochambeau
under date of July 31, 1786, he writes:

"The treaty of amity which has lately taken place between the King of Prussia and the United States marks a
new era in negotiation. It is the most liberal treaty,
which has ever been entered into between independent
powers. It is perfectly original in many of its articles;
and should its principles be considered hereafter as the
basis of connection between nations, it will operate more
fully to produce a genial pacification, than any measure
hitherto attempted amongst mankind."

In a similar strain he wrote to Lafayette, August 15, 1786.

This treaty as elaborated in the treaty of 1799
and 1828, with some modifications was still in
effect in 1917 when we entered the World War.[26]

[24] Marshall, *Washington*, V, 770, 771.
[25] *Washington's Writings*, ix, 182.
[26] "By the Treaty of Berlin, 1799, still in force, the United States
of America and the King of Prussia solemnly pledge themselves," etc.
General Orders No. 106, France, July 6, 1918, signed General Pershing.

Possibly Washington had some inkling that Frederick had not only scorned an English offer of alliance against the colonies, but that "partly by immense bribes to Panin (the Russian prime minister), Frederick had kept Catherine true to the existing political system, and had contributed to prevent Russian assistance from being given to England during the American struggle."[27]

[27] Hassall, *Balance of Power*, 1715-1789, 338.   On this subject see also Fiske, *American Revolution*, II, 143 *et seq.*, and Bancroft, *United States*, final ed., VI, ch. xxxii.   See also Schrader, *Prussia and the United States; Frederick the Great's Influence on the American Revolution.*

CHAPTER VII

The Germans Penetrate into the South and
West and Attempt Settlements in Maine and
Massachusetts — The "German Coast" of Lou-
isiana — A Texan Tragedy — Bordermen and
Pathfinders — Conrad Weiser

AT the outbreak of the Revolutionary war Virginia contained more Germans than any other
colony, excepting Pennsylvania and possibly New
York. Numerous towns in Virginia were founded
by Germans: for instance, Stephensburg, or Newton, in Frederick County, by Peter Stephens; and
Shepherdstown, first called Mecklenburg, Jefferson County, 1762, by Colonel Schaefer. A vessel
with German immigrants landed in Hampton
Roads in 1745. The Germans by degrees settled
all the valleys within a radius of 60 miles around
Peeked Mountain, so that this section received an
unmixed German character. The German church
at Winchester in the Shenandoah Valley is one of
the oldest in the country. After the Revolution a
large group of Hessians settled there. In 1734
a number of German Lutheran communities were
flourishing in Northern Virginia, and in a work

dealing with Virginian conditions that appeared in London in 1724, Governor Spotswood is mentioned as having founded the town of Germanna, named for the Germans whom Queen Anne had sent over. Col. William Byrd, a man of education and wealth, who lived on his Virginia estate in a style of great magnificence, mentions a visit to Germanna where Spotswood resided: "This famous Town consists of Col. Spotswood's enchanted Castle on one Side of the Street, and a Baker's Dozen of ruinous Tenements on the other, where so many German Familys had dwelt some Years ago; but are now remov'd ten Miles higher, in the Fork of the Rapahannock, on Land of their Own."[1]

Many Germans immigrated to the Carolinas from Germany as well as from Pennsylvania before the Revolution. Many came from Pennsylvania in 1745, and in 1751 the Mennonites bought 900,000 acres from the English government in North Carolina and founded numerous settlements, which still survive. One colony was on the Yadkin, known as the Buffalo Creek Colony.

When German immigration into South Carolina began is a matter of dispute, but when a

---

[1] Hart, *American History Told by Contemporaries*, II, 235. One work mentions a colony of Germans from the Palatinate who had been presented with a large section of land and who were prosperous, happy and exceedingly hospitable.

colony of immigrants from Salzburg reached Charleston in 1743, they found there German settlers by whom they were heartily welcomed. As early as 1674 many Lutherans, doubtless including Germans, to escape religious prejudices in New York, settled along the Ashley, near the future site of Charleston.[2]

It is probable, from printed evidence, that the first German in South Carolina was Rev. Peter Fabian, who accompanied an expedition sent by the English Carolina Company to that colony in 1663.

In 1732, under the leadership of John Peter Purry, 170 German-Swiss founded Purrysburg on the Savannah River, and were followed in a year or two by 200 more. Orangeburg was founded about the same time by Germans from Switzerland and the Palatinate. Likewise Lexington was founded by Germans, and in 1742 Germans founded a settlement on the island of St. Simons, south of Savannah. In 1763 two shiploads of German immigrants arrived at Charleston from London. Before the Revolution the Gospel was preached in sixteen German churches in the colony, and at

---

[2] Faust, op. cit., I, 215. Religious intolerance was not confined to New York. Goebel, *Deutschtum in Nord Amerika*, 11, writes: "Like the Puritan church in New England, the High Church exercised its intolerance in Virginia by excluding Catholics and sectarians from settlement and later even prohibited German Lutheran ministers from performing marriage ceremonies."

the outbreak of the Revolution the German Fusiliers was the name given to an organization of German and German-Swiss volunteers which still exists.   As early as 1766 a German Society was founded in Charleston and numbered upward of 199 members at the beginning of the Revolution. It gave 2,000 pounds to the patriot cause, and after the conclusion of peace erected its own school, at which annually twenty children of the poor were taught free of charge.   Griffis speaks of the ship "Phoenix," from New York, "which brought Germans, who built Jamestown on the Stone River."[2]

Many of the Palatine Germans and Swiss had already settled in the Carolinas; now into Georgia came Germans from farther East, besides many of the Moravians.   From the Austrian Salzburg 30,000 of these Bible-reading Christians had fled into Holland and England.   Being invited to settle in Georgia, they took the oath of allegiance to the British King and crossed the Atlantic Ocean.

In March, 1734, the ship "Purisburg", having on board eighty-seven Salzburgers with their ministers, arrived in the colony.   Warmly welcomed, they founded the town of Ebenezer.   The next year more of these sober, industrious and strongly religious people came over from Germany.   The

---

[2] *Romance of American Colonization,* 171.

Moravians, who followed quickly, began missionary work among the Indians. After them again followed German Lutherans, Moravians, English immigrants, Scotch, Irish, Quakers, Mennonites, and others. "Thus in Georgia, as in the Carolinas and Virginia, there was formed a miniature New Europe, having a varied population, with many sterling qualities."[4]

The first white people to settle within the territory comprising the present State of Ohio were the German Moravians who founded the towns of Schoenbrunn, Gnadenhutten, Lichtenau and Salem. David Zeisberger on May 3, 1772, with a number of converted Indians, founded the first Christian community in Ohio. Mrs. Johann George Jungmann was the first white married woman. She and her husband came from Bethlehem, Pa. At Schoenbrunn and Gnadenhutten, Zeisberger wrote a spelling book and reader in the Delaware language which was printed in Philadelphia. Zeisberger belongs to the class of great pioneers. President Reed of Philadelphia, in a letter to Zeisberger, thanked him, in the name of the whole country, for his services among the Indians, and particularly for his Christian humanity in turning back so many war parties on their way to rapine and massacre.

[4] *Ibid.*, 181.

In Gnadenhutten was born July 4, 1773, the
first white child in Ohio, John Ludwig Roth; the
second child was Johanna Maria Heckewelder,
born on April 16, 1781, at Schoenbrunn, and the
third, Christian David Seusemann, at Salem, May
30, 1781. The Communities composed largely of
baptized Indians, in 1775 numbered 414 persons,
and their record of industry and peaceful development is preserved in Zeisberger's diary, now in the
archives of the Historical and Philosophical
Society of Ohio at Cincinnati.

These peaceful settlements excited the jealousy
of powerful interests, and the British commissioners, McKee and Elliot, and the renegade,
Simon Girty, reported to the commander at De-
troit that Zeisberger and his flock were American spies. The German settlers and their Indian
converts were carried to Sandusky in 1781, where
they suffered great privations until permitted,
after winter had come, to send back 150 of their
Indian wards—all of whom spoke the German
language—to gather what of their planting still
remained in the fields. But a number of lawless
American bordermen under Col. David William-
son, acting on a false report that the peaceful
Indians had been concerned in a raid, surprised
the men in the fields, and after disarming them
by a trick, murdered men, women and children in

cold blood.[5] The details are among the most ghastly on record and make the blood run cold. Some of those slain had German fathers and all were peaceful, industrious, well-behaved natives who had learned to sing Christian hymns and German folk-songs in their humble meeting house. It is a striking fact in the early annals of our history that the frontier settlements teemed with Germans, and that numerous Indian massacres and many border fights with the French, before the Revolution as well as after, bring into prominence German names.[6]

Independent of these communities, the first settlement in Ohio, at Marietta, was the work of New Englanders (April, 1788); but the second, that of Columbia, now a part of Cincinnati, was under the direction of a German Revolutionary officer, Major Benjamin Steitz, the name being later changed by his descendants to Stites. In

[5] Cf. Eickhoff, *In der Neuen Heimath*, 256-262; Roosevelt, *Winning of the West*, II, ch. v.
[6] In defense of the borders against French and Indians, forts were built by the German settlers above Harrisburg at the forks of the Schuylkill, on the Lehigh and the upper Delaware. They bore the brunt of the Tulpehocken massacre in 1755, soon after Braddock's defeat; the barbarities perpetrated in Northampton County in 1756, and the attack on the settlements near Reading in 1763. Against these forays the Germans under Schneider and Hiester made stout resistance. "Among the greatest sufferers were the German settlers, especially in Berks and Northampton Counties. Hundreds were slain and scalped, houses, barns and crops went up in flames, children and women were carried into captivity. The letters of Conrad Weiser, Mühlenberg and others give many harrowing details of scenes which were then of almost daily occurrence." Kuhns, *German and Swiss Settlements*, 200.

1773 Frankfort, Kentucky, was settled mainly by German immigrants from North Carolina. In 1777 Col. Shepherd (Schaefer), a Pennsylvania German, successfully defended Wheeling against a large Indian force. In the operations under General Irvine to avenge the massacre of the Moravians in Ohio, his adjutant, Col. Rose, was a German, namely Baron Gustav von Rosenthal.

. . . . . .

In the South, Law's Mississippi Scheme brought thousands of Germans from the Palatinate, who made settlements throughout the then French colonies. French reports of the year 1687 noted by Parkman mention the presence of a German in La Salle's last expedition, that to Texas, but the first German settlers along the lower Mississippi date from 1720. The success of French colonization along the Mississippi depended on establishing permanent settlements of agriculturists, and the hope that had been centered on French settlers having miscarried, as these calculated on quick gains through the discovery of gold and silver, fur trading, etc., John Law, the Scotch financier who expected to pay France's debts through the operations of the Compagnies des Indes, turned to Switzerland and the Rhenish districts. Pamphlets in various languages were issued, one of which, printed in German, described the country in extravagantly glowing colors and contained extracts from enthusiastic letters attributed to actual settlers. A copy of this pamphlet was discovered by Professor Deiler of Tulane University in a New Orleans bookshop. It had been published in Leipzig in 1720. According to its descriptions, the Mississippi extended northward to the pole; the country was so productive that it bore four crops annually; 300 acres of land worth 30,000 thalers could be bought for 100 thalers, etc. As conditions along the Rhine and in the Palatinate were well nigh intolerable, following the Thirty Years War and the devastations committed by the armies of Louis XIV, it was not surprising that thousands of persons resolved to exchange Europe for America. Accordingly the exodus to the English colonies was followed by the emigration of at least 10,000 from the Rhine and the Palatinate whose destination was the French settlements on the Mississippi.

Their experience differed but little from that of their countrymen who took ship for New York. Owing to a woeful lack of transportation facilities, the emigrants were obliged to wait months in French ports for vessels to carry them, and, thanks to lack of provisions and epidemic diseases, their ranks were soon decimated. Then followed the long, distressful journey and long delays at San Domingo, with infections from tropical diseases. Four vessels that sailed on January 24, 1721, from L'Orient for Louisiana, had 1,200 emigrants on board, of whom only 200 arrived at their destination. The remainder were swept away by disease. The result of all this was that of about 8,000 Germans that set sail from European ports in 1720-21, not more than a third disembarked at Biloxi and Mobile.

Nor was this the end of their sorrows. There were no accommodations for them when they reached their destination. Agriculture was unknown; only a few gardens existed; the settlers received their supplies from France or from San Domingo, and if the ships failed to arrive, soldiers were sent out to fish or to scour the woods for game. Accordingly a state of semi-starvation prevailed even in normal times, which culminated in terrible conditions when the immigrants arrived, nearly half of them dying in the two ports, Biloxi and Mobile, during 1720 and 1721. Seemingly the directors of the Compagnie des Indes took the "engagés" for cattle. Their culpability was the greater because better conditions could have been obtained. For example, while the Germans were allowed to perish on one side of the river, the wreck of a provision ship on the other side was left uninspected for nearly eleven months.

Then came Law's end even before the settlers on his concession on the Arkansas River had become fairly warm. No help for the colonists whatever was now forthcoming; months elapsed following the collapse of Law's scheme before the directors decided the fate of the settlements, so that the people, when the aid derived from the Indians no longer availed, resolved to take matters into their own hands, go down the Mississippi to New Orleans and call the officials of the company to account. The flotilla having reached its destination, they demanded free transportation back to Europe. Governor Bienville did his best to persuade them by friendly means to remain, and since the 169 malcontents outnumbered the entire population of New Orleans, this proved the most judicious course. As a result of the conference, the Germans were assigned to rich alluvial lands on the right bank of the Mississippi, about twenty-five miles above New Orleans. The district, still known as the German Coast, was already occupied by two German settlements. By way of additional satisfaction, the agent on the Arkansas was dismissed and a supply of food sufficient for the winter was sent to the forty-seven persons who had remained behind.

Of the two earlier German settlements on the German Coast one dates from 1721. The year in which the other was founded, "le premier ancien village allemand," is not known, but Deiler assumes that a party of Germans arriving in 1719 by Les Deux Frères, apparently possessed of means, is entitled to this distinction.[7] The two original settlements, however, were abandoned in 1721 when a storm that lasted five days and almost destroyed New Orleans swept the waters of the Mississippi over the tilled fields and ruined the entire planting. The settlers retired to the somewhat more elevated ground overlooking the river and only seventeen families chose to remain on the original site of the two settlements.

The hardships of these German cultural pioneers in Louisiana were the most distracting imaginable. The land was covered with a thick, primeval, semi-tropical forest and with an undergrowth more impenetrable than that of the northern forests. To this was added the malarial influence of the river bottoms and the floods. The company supplied neither horses nor plows, nor means of transportation; nothing but axes, picks and spades. There was not a horse in the settlement until ten years later. The census of 1724 records but seven cows to 56 German families. Every foot of the hard soil had to be made arable by hand labor. It was therefore not astonishing

---

[7] *Settlement of the German Coast of Louisiana, 50.*

that the French "engagés" simply deserted. Deiler declares that the German settlers must inevitably have perished had they come of a less hardy stock.

A high official tribute to their endurance and the value of their pioneer labors in Louisiana appears in a letter that Laussat, the French governor, addressed to the Minister of the Interior, Chaptal, in which he heartily approves the sending of Germans to the French colony:

"This class of peasants, and especially of that nationality, is just the class we need and the only one which always achieved perfect success in these parts. What is called here the 'German Coast' is the most industrious, the most populous, the most at ease, the most upright, the most respected part of the inhabitants of this colony. . . . The emigrants of our southern provinces are not worth anything."[2]

The Germans on the German Coast received accessions at later periods, first through the soldiers of the Swiss companies, mostly Germans under Swiss officers, who settled there on the expiration of their enlistments, and in 1754 some natives of Lorraine arrived, while in 1774 a large number of German families came from Maryland.

The descendants of these first settlers, down to

[2] *Ibid.*, 129. "I regard the Germans and Canadians as the founders of all our settlements in Louisiana." *Report on Conditions in Louisiana*, Champigny, quoted by Goebel, 17.

1803, creoles of German ancestry, still form a large part of the population of the German Coast and the parishes of St. Charles and St. John the Baptist. Beyond these limits they are found along the Mississippi to the early southern boundary of the United States, outnumbering the French creoles, since the Germans had larger families than the French. In course of time they ceased to identify themselves as Germans; most of them changed their names in order to give them a French sound, but in many families the German traditions are still kept alive.

. . . . . .

The history of German immigration into Texas is of a peculiarly pathetic character which can here be considered only in general outlines. Until the founding of Austin, a settlement on the Colorado River sponsored by a Baron von Bostrop in 1823, formed the northernmost white outpost in the Colorado Valley. The settlers, chiefly from Oldenburg, were exposed to frequent Indian raids and repeatedly compelled to abandon their homesteads for periods of variable duration. In the early '40s, a number of Germans, Alsatians and Swiss arrived in Texas under the leadership of a Frenchman named Henri Castro, who had a contract to settle a section near San Antonio and founded Castroville. We find that a Teutonia

Order existed in Austin as early as 1841 to promote immigration and preserve contact with Germany. But already toward the close of the second
and the beginning of the third decennial, German
families were established between the Brazos and
the Colorado.

The war for the liberation of Texas brought a
number of young German volunteers who settled
in Texas after the revolution. An association
calling itself Germania was formed in New York
City in 1839 to found a colony in Texas, and a
vanguard of 130 persons set sail November 2d
of that year in the brig North, but dissolved
soon after reaching Houston, the majority faring
miserably.

Soon a rage for speculation in Mexican and
Texas land-grants broke out, and the promoters
turned to Germany as the most promising field
for recruiting settlers in order to make their
grants a source of profit. And this forms the beginning of a chapter of peculiar interest in the
history of German immigration.

Early in the '40s, Count von Castell, an adjutant of the Duke of Nassau, conceived the idea
of concentrating German immigration at a selected spot in Texas. A group of petty princes
and respected nobles was persuaded to form an
association for this purpose and induced to sub-

scribe a considerable sum of money toward carrying it into effect. Count Joseph von Boos-Waldeck and Victor von Leiningen were commissioned to undertake a tour of inspection, and Boos established a flourishing plantation on Jack Creek. On the strength of Leiningen's favorable report, the Association, calling itself the Corporation of Nobles of Mayence, published a prospectus recommending the locality selected as specially suited to German settlement. The first negotiations were entrusted to a French adventurer, and then, after his true character had been revealed, to one Henry Fischer of Cassel and a former resident of Texas, who entered into a contract for a large area of land on the San Saba River for $16,000, with a share in the profits; and the Association promised, in consideration of the payment of 300 guldens for one person and of 600 guldens for a family, to transport free of charge to Texas, those that desired to take advantage of the offer, and to furnish a blockhouse, 160 acres of land to each adult male immigrant, 320 to each family, and horses, cattle and farming implements at cost price, besides the eventual building of a church, schoolhouses, apothecaries and a hospital. The conditions were that each man must break fifteen acres of land and occupy his house. Incidentally the plan contemplated the establishment of an independent colony within the Republic of Texas, and this plan was said to be secretly favored by England, which frowned upon the prospective annexation of Texas to the American Union.

Prince Carl zu Solms-Braunfels in May, 1844, as Commissioner-General, departed for the scene of his future activities and was followed presently by three sailing ships with 150 families, who embarked at Bremen at the cost of the Association. They arrived at the port of Indianola (Lavacca) in December, and, driving ox-carts, embarked upon a journey of unspeakable hardships over trackless paths and through treacherous swamps, exposed to frequent attacks from the Indians. They did not arrive at their destination until the end of March, 1845. Here on the Comal River Solms had acquired 1,000 acres for the founding of a town as the first relay-station for those that were to follow. Meanwhile it was discovered that the land purchased by Fischer, represented to have an extent of 400 miles, was too remote from the coast and inaccessible from other settlements. The new town was staked out on the high banks of the Comal River and called Neu-Braunfels.

For a while all went well. The men applied themselves diligently to the task of improving their allotments, happy to be located at last, and even a second contingent of immigrants that fol-

lowed fared tolerably well, as the Association had
sent means sufficient to provide for the expense of
their journey and for their support. But the
headless management of affairs in Texas suffered
serious embarrassment when the remittances from
home became more and more sparing. Commissioner-General Solms, having squandered much
money and being appalled by the enormity of the
difficulties with which the enterprise was hedged
about, resigned and returned home, and the
Colonial Council that had been created to assist
him passed out of existence.

The future looked desperate, but thanks to the
policy of strict economy and rigid management
which the newly-arrived director, Baron von
Meusebach, put into effect, the settlement survived, and in the fall of 1845 Meusebach selected
about ninety miles from Neu-Braunfels an area
of several thousand acres for an additional settlement, which subsequently became known as Friedrichsburg (Fredericksburg).

Meanwhile several thousand immigrants had
arrived at Galveston; but when Meusebach arrived
there to provide for their comfort and to send
them to their destination, he was appalled to discover that the Association had sent no money with
which to defray the expenses, and families that
had made deposits of money with the Association,

with the understanding that it would be paid back to them when they arrived at Galveston, suddenly found themselves penniless and in want. Months were to elapse before their property would be returned to them. Meusebach hastened to New Orleans in the hope of raising money, and by degrees the immigrants were shipped from Galveston to Indian Point on Lavacca Bay, where their real troubles were now to begin.

Eickhoff writes that the contents of the collected documents, with the promises of the Association, appeared in Texas, on the scene of naked reality, more like a tale from the Arabian Nights than a solemn engagement of sane men. Of the 2500 passengers who had left Germany, about 2300 landed at Galveston, and about fifty men were sent to the "colony". The rest either lay at Indian Point, some camping in the open, some in tents, or in Galveston in three enormous wooden sheds, waiting for "the roads to improve" and told that the money due them would be paid at Neu-Braunfels.[*]

Indian Point (Indianola) consisted of a single house situated on the steep, sandy bluffs of Lavacca Bay. Several large frame sheds were erected, into which as many of the immigrants as possible were crowded for shelter; the rest lived

---

[*] Eickhoff, *In der Neuen Heimath*, 327.

in tents. Wind and rain, lack of wood and fresh water, and mosquito and malaria-breeding pools made existence a burden, while the ensuing long period of idleness, coupled with harrowing anxieties as to the future, exercised a frightfully depressing as well as demoralizing effect on the people. All conditions existed to produce climatic diseases and epidemics. The rate of mortality increased appallingly. At last a general cry of despair arose—the place must be abandoned!

Here unexpected obstacles arose. War with Mexico had been declared; all means of transportation had been requisitioned for the carrying of war material, provisions, etc. Although Meusebach had entered into contracts with merchants at Houston for the removal of the immigrants, the agreements could not be carried out, in part because the unusually protracted rains had rendered the roads along the coast impassable, and the oxen-drawn wagons that started were stalled for weeks because they could not cross the swollen rivers and streams. In desperation, hopeless of escaping from the death-stricken spot by any other means, several hundred men organized an independent command and entered the war against Mexico.

Only a few hundred still remained at Indian Point in the fall of 1846. One-third of the origi-

recital of the experience of the martyrs of Indian
Point, many new immigrants set out for Texas in
the years following, and in the early '50s the State
possessed a large, well-to-do German population
which continued to increase at a steady rate until
the Civil War.   Neu-Braunfels profited materially
by the exodus following the German revolution of
1848-49, as also did Friedrichsburg.   Among
those who moved to Texas after the catastrophe
of 1846 was one who was destined to play an
important political rôle before and after the Civil
War — Gustav Schleicher, who became widely
known in the United States Congress for his
statesmanlike views and knowledge.

.   .   .   .   .   .

German immigration into Maryland began in
1732 under Augustin Herrmann, and contributed
materially to the upbuilding of that colony, the
population of which numbered about 32,000, including negroes.   Herrmann arrived in America
from German Bohemia in 1643.   He attained
prominence in the colony of New Netherland and
was sent on a diplomatic mission into Maryland
in 1660 by Peter Stuyvesant.   Under a commission from Cecil Calvert he prepared a compre-
hensive and accurate map of Maryland that was
sent to England to be printed and was pronounced
by the king to be the best map he had ever seen.   In

consideration of his valuable work, Herrmann in 1663 received a patent to 5,000 acres of land in Cecil County which was settled by Germans. One of these Maryland Germans was Johann Lederer, a man of superior educational and linguistic accomplishments, endowed with indomitable courage and a restless spirit of adventure. He was appointed by Governor Berkeley of Virginia to head an expedition to discover a pass through the Blue Ridge and Alleghany Mountains to India, a project then thought feasible. Lederer recorded his remarkable adventures in a book written in Latin, which was translated by Lord Talbot and published in London in 1672.

When Charles Calvert, fifth Lord Baltimore, in 1732, issued his proclamation offering liberal inducements to settlers on the lands between the Susquehanna and Potomac rivers, streams of immigrants began to pour in over the Blue Ridge mountains, a large number of whom were Germans from Pennsylvania; they settled in western Maryland which in 1760 boasted of having eight German churches. In 1739 Jonathan Hager with a number of others from Germany settled in what is now Washington County, and in 1762 Hager laid out a townsite which he named Elizabeth-Town in honor of his wife. In 1813 the name was changed to Hagerstown. As a German immigrant he was ineligible to election as a member of the Assembly, but he was twice chosen, twice unseated and twice re-elected. The Assembly passed an enabling act that was forwarded to Lord Baltimore by Governor Eden with his recommendation, in which he speaks in terms of high praise of the Germans, saying that their conversion of the wilderness into well-stocked plantations, the example and beneficent effects of their extraordinary industry, have raised in no small degree a spirit of emulation among the other inhabitants. Prince Bernhard of Weimar in 1825 described Frederickstown, a German settlement, as "one of the principal places in the state of Maryland, and is situated in a well-cultivated country surrounded by hills. It has about five thousand inhabitants."[10]

The first printing office in Baltimore was established by Nicholas Hasselbach in 1764, and was the forerunner of the *Baltimore American*, still a prominent newspaper. In 1795 Samuel Sauer, a son of Christopher Sauer, the first publisher of the Bible in a European tongue on the American continent, established a type foundry in association with William Gwinn, which laid the foundation of the American Typefoundry Company of to-day; he also published a large number of books.

The earliest German settlements in Maryland

[10] *Travels in North America*, I, 184.

were Frederickstown, Hagerstown and Middletown. Frederickstown was founded by Thomas Schley, the ancestor of Admiral Schley, a schoolmaster, who settled there in 1735 with one hundred Palatine and German Swiss families. Pastor Schlatter in the story of his travels (1746-1751) wrote: "It is the great advantage for this congregation that they have the best schoolmaster I have met with in America."[11]

One of the first settlements in New Jersey was that of German Valley, extending through Morris and Hunterdon counties, where a congregation of the Reformed Church, coming from between Wolfenbuttel and Halberstadt in Germany, settled in 1705. Early German communities existed in Sommerset, Sussex, Passaic, Bergen and Essex counties.

The New England States made efforts to get German settlers and issued official invitations and promises. Accordingly German Reformed and Lutheran congregations purchased a tract of land from one General Waldo and founded Waldoborough, in what is now Maine and was then a part of Massachusetts. The name of the adjacent county of Bremen and that of the town of Frankfort on the Penobscot point to early German settlements. In 1746 Canadian Indians attacked

[11] Faust, *op. cit.*, I, 169.

Waldoborough and destroyed it root and branch. As the colonial government of Massachusetts promised protection and aid to German immigrants, because, as they declared, the Germans among them had introduced many useful trades and arts, some thirty more families arrived in 1751, and in the following year 1,500 additional immigrants settled on the west side of the Muscongus, Broadbay and Broadcove. But the Germans seemed destined not to prosper on New England soil, for in 1755 the settlements were again attacked by Indians and devastated. The survivors had hardly recovered from this visitation and restored the flourishing condition of their fields when Waldo died. The charter that he had issued to the Germans was not respected after his death, as others asserted a prior claim to the land. It was the history of the Palatines in New York over again. Some sixty families were forced to pay for their property a second time, whereupon a still older title was unearthed and put in evidence against theirs, until, weary of such intrigues, they sold their property for a song and joined their countrymen in Orangeburg in South Carolina. A number subsequently returned to Maine.

Germans also settled in Massachusetts proper by official invitation of the assembly in 1749.

These were intended, with others to follow, to be the founders of a system of industrial ventures in the colony. Negotiations were actually opened with an attorney named Luther and an agreement was entered into under which he and his country-men were to be paid for the work of carrying out extensive plans for a manufacturing system, and an attempt was made to start a German manufac-turing town at Braintree near Boston. But the matter turned out badly and the Germans were left to shift for themselves.

. . . . . .

Neither in New York, Pennsylvania nor in the South did the Germans shirk the dangers and hardships of the wilderness. It is not generally appreciated how large a share they had in the settling of the West. They poured into Ohio from the Mohawk Valley as well as from Penn-sylvania. On the dark and bloody ground of Kentucky they vied with Daniel Boone in clearing the land of the Indians. One of the most famous among the pioneers was "the tall Dutchman," George Yeager (Jaeger), who was killed by In-dians in 1775. In the Valley of Virginia there were probably more German pioneers than of any other nationality. Along the whole border from New England to Georgia they occupied advanced posts in the enemy's country, and a Kentucky observer declared at the close of the eighteenth century that of every twelve families, nine Germans, seven Scotchmen and four Irishmen succeeded when all others failed.[12]   Michael Fink and his companions were the first to descend the Mississippi on a trading expedition to New Orleans, where the officials in 1782 had never heard of Pittsburg, their starting point.   Germans again, Rosenvelt, Becker and Heinrich, were the first to descend the Ohio in a steamboat, 1811.[13]

The history of the early border troubles brings into relief the names of numerous Germans who either as rangers, interpreters, negotiators or missionaries were true pathfinders.   American history cannot ignore the great service rendered by the Moravian Brotherhood and particularly by one of its illustrious members, Christian Frederick Post. Next to Weiser, he served best the interests of the settlers, and the cold-blooded massacre of the Moravian Indians in the Ohio wilderness and the ruthless destruction of the Moravian work of civilization, standing almost unparalleled in the record of border violence, seem tragic requital for his risks and sacrifices.   It was this heroic Moravian who in 1758, singly penetrating the primeval forest and facing alone a horde of savages bent on

[12] Roosevelt, op. cit., III, 17.
[13] Rosengarten, German Soldier, 124.

destroying the American settlements, successfully accomplished his mission of alienating the powerful Indian tribes from their alliance with the French and making them the allies of the English at a critical time when no Englishman dared venture upon such an expedition.[14]

Lou Wetzel was the foremost ranger and Indian fighter on the Ohio, whose exploits have been commemorated in numerous border stories of a previous generation. As a hunter and fighter there was not in all the land his superior.[15] His father, born in the Palatinate, emigrated to Pennsylvania and became an early pioneer of the West, settling probably near Wheeling, in the county of West Virginia which perpetuates the family name. Many adventures are told of Wetzel in his relentless feud against the Indians for having murdered his father. His brothers, Martin and Jacob, were likewise Indian fighters of repute.

On the upper Muskingum a Pennsylvania German, Ebenezer Zane (Zahn) founded Zanesville.

[14] A recital of his daring undertaking and thrilling experience is contained in Parkman, *Montcalm and Wolfe,* II, 144-150. "During the late bloody war all commerce between the white people and Indians being suspended, he [Post] was entrusted first by this government, and then by Brig.-Gen. Forbes, with negotiations to secure the Indian nations." *Penn. Arch., 1st Series,* III, 579. "Although a large price was set on the head of Post, he was fearless. 'I am not afraid,' he wrote, 'of the Indians nor the devil himself'." *Ibid.,* 542.

[15] Roosevelt, *op. cit.,* II, 138.

He established the first permanent foothold on the Ohio River in 1769, building a blockhouse on the present site of Wheeling. The fort was attacked in 1782 by forty British soldiers and 186 Indians. Elizabeth, the sister of Ebenezer Zane, won renown in this encounter by supplying the defenders with powder from a magazine forty yards distant, in full view of the besiegers and under a volley of rifle shots. "You haven't a man to spare," she said; "a woman will not be missed in the defense of the fort." Wheeling has erected a monument to the memory of this heroic woman.

In the village of Goshen in 1808 died at the age of eighty-seven David Zeisberger after a life spent in blazing a path for civilization through the primeval forest. The first pioneer hunters in the Blue Grass region of Kentucky, in addition to Yeager and Michael Stoner (Steiner), were John Harman (Hermann), John Haggin (Hagen), Joseph and Jacob Sodowsky (Sandusky), Peter Nieswanger, Michael Schuck, Leonard Helm, Abraham Hite and Abraham Schöplein (Chaplin).[14] Stoner and Harrod are credited with preceding Daniel Boone in hunting expeditions in Kentucky. George Yeager, "the tall Dutchman," had visited Kentucky when as a boy he was captured by Indians. Kasper Mansker, or Mansco,

---

[14] Faust, *op. cit.*, I, 378, quoting *Der Deutsche Pionier*, X, 273.

was one of the most famous of Indian fighters, a wonderful marksman and woodsman.[17] He was made a colonel of the frontier militia. The crack of his deadly rifle, "Nancy", haunted his foes like a message of doom. The German family of Poe were noted as Indian fighters in the middle period.

A typical border ranger of an earlier period was John Adam Hartmann. With Timothy Murphy, he was the most relentless Indian fighter in the Mohawk Valley. Murphy married the daughter of a well-to-do German settler, John Fink, after the Revolution and settled down to the life of an orderly farmer, but Hartmann ended his life in an almshouse. He had admittedly been a poacher in his own country, the Palatinate, and escaped to America, where he turned hunter and frontiersman. Hartmann surpassed all his countrymen in endurance, vigilance and speed of foot. He was a giant in stature and endowed with tremendous strength. When the Revolution broke out he was famed as one of the best shots in the valley, and when Sir John Johnson turned the Indians against his former neighbors, Hartmann became their relentless enemy, lying in wait for them day and night. He had neither home nor family, but he found a hearty welcome in every German cabin. Mothers felt safe when they knew of his pres-

[17] *Ibid.*, I, 368, citing Roosevelt, *op. cit.*, I, 150, and Carr, *Early Times in Middle Tennessee.*

ence in the neighborhood; the children played un-
concernedly in the open if John Adam had been
observed by them during the day, and the farmer
went to his work without fear, knowing the
ranger to be not far off, assured that his rifle
would give timely warning of approaching danger.
How many Indians he killed is not known, for
Hartmann disliked to talk about the subject, but
among those who paid the penalty of their crimes
was a redoubtable Indian who, after the war,
boasted in Hartmann's presence that he had killed
many German settlers and displayed a tobacco
pouch made of the skin taken from the arm of a
white child.

To the ancestry of President Harding is credited, in an authorized biographical sketch issued
a few days before the election of 1920, a German
pioneer. This progenitor of the American Hard-
ings was Joshua Dickerson (of German parentage), the second child born in Monmouth County,
N. J. His life being that of the adventurous
pioneer, is conspicuous in settlers' history. "He
was the first white man to scale the Alleghanies,"
settling temporarily on the Maryland side of the
Potomac, says the sketch. Finally, after a roving
and adventurous career, he, with his wife
(Susana Whitten) and fourteen children, took
root in what is now Fayette County, on Dicker-

son Run, Pa. Early in 1800 his grandson, Thomas, great-grandfather of the President on the maternal side, left Fayette County and went to Ohio to join an early Methodist settlement, where he cleared land and built a cabin. The mother of President Cleveland was the daughter of an Irish bookseller and a German Quakeress.

With Post, preeminent among German pioneers, and the peer of the most noted and important American pathfinders, ranks Conrad Weiser, the son of Johann Conrad Weiser, leader of the New York Palatines and founder of Weiserdorf. He reached the shores of the new world at the age of thirteen. Young Weiser at once ingratiated himself into the confidence of the Indians and with his father's consent was adopted by Quagnant, a Mohawk chief, who taught him the Indian language. This training in later years made him one of the foremost men in the history of the frontier. Expert in Indian lore, speaking the tongue of the Six Nations, by his influence with the Indians on the one hand and with the colonial governments of Pennsylvania, New York, Maryland, Virginia and Carolina, on the other, he succeeded in deferring the alliance between the French and Indians until the American colonists had grown strong enough to defend themselves

successfully.[18]   In more than one crisis he retained
the confidence of the Six Nations and the Southern
Indians, and although a lasting peace was never
made between the Indian confederacies, Weiser so
managed the Six Nations as to reduce hostilities to
a minimum. It was he that guided the Indian policy
of the provinces, and in the words of his biogra-
pher, for twenty-five years held the Iroquois aloof
from the French while he prevented Virginia and
Carolina from bringing on a war with this powerful confederation.   "And all these years were
needed to enable the English to win the victory
which swept French dominion from North America
in 1763."[19]

During his active career no extensive Indian
uprisings occurred, and he is described by Lossing
as "the first who combined the activity of a
pioneer with the outlook of a statesman."   Washington said of him: "Posterity will not forget his
just deserts."   He was at once the ablest and
shrewdest interpreter in the employ of the English
and was generally regarded a man of extraordinary character, being inspired both by the spirit
of adventure and by deep religious feelings.   His
journey to the Ohio in 1748 was the first of an
official character to the West across the Appa-

[18] *Harper's Encyclopedia of United States History*, X, 302.
[19] Walton, *Conrad Weiser*, 13.

lachian range, and not without truth has Weiser
been called the true western pathfinder.

Weiser also served the provincial government
as commander of the border forts during the
French and Indian War and his German countrymen as leader and councilor in political, religious
and school affairs. His daughter married Heinrich Melchior Mühlenberg, the founder of the
Lutheran Church in America. His grandsons
were General Peter Mühlenberg and Frederick
August Mühlenberg, the first serving as vice
president of the State of Pennsylvania in 1785
(Benjamin Franklin being president), and as
representative in Congress for three terms, and
the latter being elected Speaker of the Pennsylvania State Legislature, a member of the first four
Congresses and Speaker of the House in the First
and the Third Congresses of the United States.
A third grandson, G. H. E. Mühlenberg became
noted as a botanist. A great grandson was Rev.
William Augustus Mühlenberg, founder of St.
Luke's Hospital, New York, born in Philadelphia in 1796. During his first rectorship at Lancaster, Pa., he was instrumental in establishing the
first public schools outside of Philadelphia. While
at Flushing, Long Island, he founded a school,
afterwards St. Paul's College, and subsequently
also the first Protestant sisterhood in the United

States, crowning his life's work by organizing St. Johnsland on the north shore of Long Island, a home for destitute and crippled children, an old men's home, etc. He was the author of the popular Protestant hymn, "I would not live alway." His death occurred in 1877.

CHAPTER VIII

Development of the American National Character — Influence of the Germans and Irish — Stephen A. Douglas and the Nebraska Bill — Campaigns of 1854-56—Lincoln and the Germans — 1860.

GERMAN immigration in the early stages is composed of the better peasant class, upon whom evil days had fallen in their native land; many, however, respectable burghers who had become impoverished successively by the Thirty Years War and the ravages of Louis XIV. Thus we know that Conrad Weiser's grandfather and father had occupied the position of magistrate in their community and that the family was fairly well-to-do. H. M. M. Richards declares that in the course of his genealogical researches, embracing many of the early German immigrants, he was astonished to find how large a number of them sprang from patrician families, even from those of the higher ranks of the nobility. "Indeed I question whether the percentage of emigrants of eminent family descent, in Pennsylvania, was not greater

amongst the Germans than those of any other
nationality, and it is a fact, beyond peradventure
that the remaining portion, the peasantry, were
unequalled, as a class, in every characteristic necessary for the founding and upbuilding of a great
nation. Even the despised 'Redemptioners' of
later years, whose status has been so grossly mis-
understood and perverted, were no exceptions to
the general rule."[1]

The character of the immigration following the
Napoleonic wars, continuing until the German
revolution of 1848 and down to the Civil War, as
already indicated, was marked by features typical
of German social, business and intellectual life,
and exerted an incalculable influence in steadying,
modifying as well as refining the restless spirit
that was extant following the French and Indian
and Revolutionary wars, the turbulent trend of
national expansion and the quest of adventure that
led to the rapid settling of the West.

It would be a gross delusion to assume with
various nativistic historians that the character of
the American people had been fixed in its present-
day attributes and features at the time of the
Revolution, or even before. It would also be an
erroneous assumption to take for granted that the
motley colonial population had crystallized into a

[1] *German Leaven,* 7.

nation in the turn of a hand. The American national character in its highest form is neither that of the typical New Englander nor that of the former slave and plantation owner, but rather is expressed in the type produced by the conquest of the West. And its very face is lined with German characteristics. Above all, the boundless individualism and soaring idealism is a Germanic inheritance. The American national character developed slowly to its present state during the last decennials of the eighteenth and the early decennials of the nineteenth centuries, not along the Atlantic seaboard where the inhabitants continued more or less to perpetuate European traditions, but in the primeval forests and on the rolling prairies and boundless plains where the settlers were forced to return to the early stages of civilization and to live again in short order through the separate periods of communal and State construction. This "return to nature" in the widest sense explains the indestructible vitality of youth of the American people that has astounded all Europe. And many of the leaders of the successful invasion of the West, beginning with the middle of the eighteenth century, were Germans.[2]

Fiske declares that the result of the partial union of the two great streams of immigration

[2] Goebel, *Das Deutschtum in den Vereinigten Staaten,* 39.

composed of the Scotch-Irish and Palatines "influenced South Carolina and Maryland most powerfully, completely renovated society in North Carolina, and broke down the sway of the Cavalier aristocracy in Virginia. While it sent southward men and women enough to accomplish all this, enough more remained in Pennsylvania to form more than half the population, raising it before 1770 to third place among the thirteen colonies, next after Virginia and Massachusetts. From the same prolific hive came the pioneers of Kentucky and Tennessee, with their descendants throughout the Mississippi Valley and beyond. In all these directions[3] this sturdy population, distilled through the Pennsylvania alembic, has formed the main strength of American democracy, and its influence upon American life has been manifold."[4]

The conception of the intellectual influence of the later German immigration may be rendered more comprehensible by citing the fact that a famous poet, Nicholaus Lenau, and at least three

---

[3] See Fiske, *Old Virginia and Her Neighbors*, II, ch. xvii.

[4] *Dutch and Quaker Colonies*, II, 355. "This immigration impressed more strongly than ever upon the middle colonies that complexity in race and religion which had been characteristic of them from the first." Greene, *Provincial America*, 234. "This population of the interior [of the Carolinas and Georgia] had entered the region in the course of the second half of the eighteenth century. Scotch-Irish and Germans passed down the Great Valley from Pennsylvania into Virginia, and through the gaps in the Blue Ridge out to the Piedmont region of the Carolinas, while contemporaneously other streams from Charleston advanced to meet them." Turner, *Rise of the New West*, p. 51.

fiction writers of international reputation in their day—Charles Sealsfield (Carl Postel), of whom Longfellow spoke as "our favorite Sealsfield"; Frederick Gerstaecker and Otto Ruppius, and other novelists, Balduin Möllhausen, Armand and Mügge, not only made propaganda for America in their fascinating tales and sketches of American frontier and backwoods life, but lived the life of the people as teachers, farmers and hunters. Indeed, there exists a distinct school of German-American literature extremely rich and varied in range, from poetry and fiction to history and science. Not only did German instructors find congenial occupation in eastern seats of learning, but in the South and West the later-day colleges welcomed them for their ability and thoroughness. In most of the newer towns and cities Germans were found engaged in teaching music and art, and along with societies for the advancement of learning were found their reading, speaking, singing and athletic clubs. An anonymous tribute to the Germans, dating back to the third decennial of the last century, declares: "There are Germans in every scientific institution, in trades and manufactories, where they invariably occupy the most important places."

Their idealism must always redound to their credit, though their too ardent devotion to spir-

itual and social detachment has led to the not unjust reproach that they are apt to cultivate comfort of mind and body at the expense of their
political duties, and in their untranslatable state
of "Gemütlichkeit" have shown relatively little
taste for political action.

A third and somewhat later class of German
immigrants may be described as industrialists,
merchants and small shop-keepers, with less of the
idealism than that inherent in the first two classes.
If the first sought homes and willingly helped to
convert the wilderness into a garden, the second
class, generally speaking, came with sufficient
means to buy homes and make them the radiating
center of cultural influences. Out of their midst
issued many distinguished writers, encyclopedists,
scientists, soldiers and patriots.

The high tide of German immigration set in
after 1840. In that decade the new arrivals numbered 434,626; in the next, 951,667; declined to
787,468 in the decade following, and reached the
apex between 1881 and 1890, when they numbered
1,452,970, after which the tide receded in con-
sonance with the phenomenal development, in-
dustrially, of the German empire. The nineteenth
century witnessed the arrival of a total of
5,009,280 Germans at American ports. The census of 1910 gives the percentage of Germans at

26.8 of the total white population (including about 3,000,000 Hollanders), or one-fourth of the American people.

A great many of the new comers between 1830 and 1870 went West and helped to people Missouri, Illinois, Indiana, Iowa, Michigan, Wisconsin and Minnesota, as well as Colorado, California, Oregon and Washington. In these States and territories not a few became prominent. If the Germans kept the State of Missouri in the Union, it was to Hermann Raster, editor of the great Chicago German daily newspaper, the *Illinois Staats Zeitung,* that Secretary Seward of President Lincoln's cabinet turned during the Civil War as his intermediary with Bismarck for the sale of a Union bond issue in Prussia to an amount aggregating hundreds of millions of dollars,[5] when England and France opposed their sale in those countries.

The German element became inspired with a new political spirit through the accession of the large influx of scholars and professional men following the failure of the German revolution of

[5] Carl Schurz said in a speech in Philadelphia, September 16, 1864: "You have heard of the people of Germany pouring their gold lavishly into the treasury of the United States (applause). You have heard of a loan of a thousand millions having been offered and being now in progress of negotiation. Would those people who are standing by us so generously in our embarrassments, would they have done so if they did not trust in our ability and determination to carry through the war?" Rhodes, *United States,* IV, 535n.

1848. The abolition movement did not at first
greatly affect them. They had well-defined views
on human slavery, but these were chiefly intuitive
and academic; they did not come into personal
contact with the institution of slavery and for.
some time maintained a detached attitude toward
it. It was not until the bill to organize the Kansas
and Nebraska territories was introduced in the
Senate by Stephen A. Douglas of Illinois that the
Germans became intensely aroused on the issue.

The measure was introduced in the session of
Congress of 1853-54. It carried out the principle
adopted in the compromise of 1850, approved by
the Whig and Democratic parties in 1851 and en-
dorsed by them in their conventions of 1852. It
defined that slavery was not to be legislated into
any State or Territory, or to be excluded there-
from, but the people thereof were to be left perfectly free to form and regulate their domestic institutions in their own way. But Douglas accepted
the amendment of Senator Dixon of Kentucky,
which flatly provided for the repeal of the Missouri Compromise and thereby opened up the vast
regions of the unsettled West to owners of slaves.
It was this action of Douglas, who until then had
been a strong favorite of the German element,
principally of the West, that turned the tide and
led to some remarkable demonstrations of temper,

notably in Chicago. At a German mass meeting
in that city in 1854, leading spokesmen among the
Germans denounced Douglas as the betrayer of
their faith, and in the frenzy of the moment a
large banner with a picture of "the little giant"
was carried in procession through the streets and
publicly burned. The conduct of the crowd
stimulated the Knownothing agitation in the Senate as well as in many localities throughout the
country, in which Douglas silently acquiesced, and
in turn it produced a state of mind among the
Germans that undoubtedly caused Douglas to lose
the Presidential election to Abraham Lincoln in
1860.

"Among the elements and forces that suddenly
came together in January, 1854," writes Professor
Herriott, "producing the 'tornado' in opposition
to the passage of the Nebraska bill that so
astonished and enraged Senator Stephen A. Douglas, the Germans constituted a factor of great
potency—much more influential than their mere
number in the population would suggest and more
important than has been realized by American
historians. The opposition of the Germans to the
passage of that celebrated measure was instant,
direct and positive; and so pronounced was their
antagonism that it became, in the writer's judgment, a decisive consideration in critical junctures

in the passage of the bill through Congress. Moreover, the tremendous disturbance thereby resulting among the Germans was a major cause of disturbing their political alignments; shaking and almost shattering their loyalty to the Democratic party, with which three fourths of the Germans were then affiliated, inducing secessions in large numbers in 1856; and it set in motion among them the forces in opposition to slavery that made the Germans a determining factor in the overthrow of the Democratic party in 1860 and in the exaltation of Abraham Lincoln."[6]

It is certainly noteworthy that practically from that day the anti-slavery sentiment, which had been acute for a period of three score and ten years, crystallized into organized party opposition and took the name of the Republican party. It nominated John C. Frémont of California.

Spurred on to action by their resentment against Knownothingism and natural hatred of slavery, the Germans, many of them trained to political independent thinking by the Revolution of 1848, threw themselves ardently into the campaign for the election of General Frémont. Frederick Hecker, the military chief of the Baden insurrection in 1849, was a candidate with Abraham Lin-

. [6] *"The Germans of Chicago and Stephen A. Douglas in 1854,"* 381. See Von Holst, IV, 426-30; Rhodes, *United States,* I, 495, Faust, II, 126-33.

coln on the Republican electoral ticket in Illinois, and spoke from the stump in his own State and in other sections. In Wisconsin, Carl Schurz was heard for the first time.[7] The defeat of Frémont was a severe disappointment to him. The next year Schurz was nominated for lieutenant-governor and defeated by 107 votes. The Know-nothings had "knifed" him. This notwithstanding, at the Chicago convention that nominated Lincoln in 1860, Schurz was chairman of the Wisconsin delegation and one of the committee appointed to notify Lincoln of the decision that had been reached by the convention.

Other German leaders were equally active, and one of the most prominent was Gustav Koerner, a personal friend of Lincoln and one of his pallbearers, lieutenant-governor of Illinois, 1853-56, and appointed by Lincoln to succeed Schurz as minister to Spain.

In the national campaign of 1856 James Buchanan, the Democratic candidate, triumphed; but a powerful progressive movement had been set in motion and new alignments were rapidly form-

[7] The father of Andrew D. White, a type of the thinking American of that period, then on the verge of the grave, closely followed the campaign literature on the slavery question which his son read to him. "Of all the speeches he best liked those of this new orator (Schurz); he preferred them, indeed, to those of his idol Seward." "His arguments seemed to me (A. D. White) by far the best of that whole campaign— the broadest, the deepest, and most convincing." White, *Autobiography*, I, 86, 87.

ing. The years 1854-56 embraced a period of
party fusion that preceded the birth of the new
party and led to the calling of a number of State
conventions to complete the organization and
formulate a national platform. A conference of
editors took place on February 22, 1856, at Decatur, Illinois, at which a program was adopted
that was to be put through the State convention
at Bloomington on May 29. At a reunion of the
survivors of that conference, held in 1900, Paul
Selby, one of the participants in the Decatur conference, related the following:

"Without disparagement to any, it is safe to
say, that Dr. Chas. H. Ray (of the *Chicago
Tribune*) and George Schneider (of the *Ill. Staats
Zeitung*) were controlling factors in forming the
platform — the former in conjunction with Mr.
Lincoln in the clear enunciation of the principles
of the new party on the subject of slavery, and the
latter as the faithful representative of the German
anti-Nebraska element, in his championship of
religious tolerance, and the maintenance of the
naturalization laws as they were, as against the
demand for the exclusion of persons of foreign
birth from the rights of American citizenship."[a]

Most of the recommendations and resolutions
then adopted were accepted by the State conven-

[a] Schneider, *Abraham Lincoln und das Deutschthum*, 66.

tion, and must thus be regarded as Lincoln's confession of the political faith which guided him.

At the first Republican national convention in Philadelphia on June 17, 1856, nineteen of the delegates were Germans. Among those that addressed the convention were George Schneider of Chicago, Francis Grimm of Belleville, Ill., and Philip Dorsheimer of Buffalo. The choice fell upon Frémont; Lincoln received 110 votes for Vice President.

In the Senatorial contest in Illinois that followed between Douglas and Lincoln, resulting in the latter's defeat, two distinguished German-Americans took the hustings for Lincoln. They were Gustav Koerner and Carl Schurz. The German element was deserting the Democratic party rapidly and among their leaders were men like Hermann Kriege and Judge Goepp of New York; Dr. Hering and the elder Seidensticker of Pennsylvania; Albert Lange and Dr. Hornburg of Indiana; H. Koch of Dubuque, Frederick Muench of Missouri and John B. Stallo of Cincinnati.

Forty-two German-born delegates appeared in the next Republican convention. Missouri sent five; Muench, Carl Bernays, Dr. Bruns, Arnold Krekel (afterwards chairman of the Missouri constitutional convention which forever abolished slavery in that State and famous as a federal judge), and Dr. A. Hammer. Illinois sent Koerner and Schneider; from Wisconsin came Carl Schurz, and from Ohio, Frederick Hassaureck. Nearly half of the Pennsylvania delegation of twenty-seven delegates were men with German names.

Lincoln was not the first choice of the Germans. The majority were adherents of Seward. But Koerner, as a member of the State Central Committee of Illinois, was a staunch Lincoln man and invariably managed, in conversation with his friends, to bring the topic to bear upon Lincoln as a compromise candidate in case of a deadlock; he used the Tremont House, a Lincoln headquarters during the Chicago convention, as a center for a silent campaign among the German delegates.

Schurz amid great applause was named with Preston King of New York to escort the permanent chairman, George Ashmun, to the platform. He had been selected to second William M. Evarts' nomination of Seward, and, together with Koerner, Bernays, Otto and Hatterschied, was a member of the committee on resolutions and platform.

In the debate on the naturalization plank, Schurz declared that 300,000 German votes had been given to the Republican party in 1856 and he hoped they would find it compatible with their honor and security again to cast 300,000 votes for the nominee of the convention. They were not only the most loyal but the most disinterested members of the Republican party, he declared. "We shall never come to you for a favor nor with expectations of reward; all we ask of you is to allow us to fight in your ranks with faith in your principles and with honor to ourselves."[9] Frederick Hassaureck followed and pledged the support of 20,000 German votes in Ohio.

Seward was first choice of a large portion of the convention, but when on the second ballot he failed to receive a majority, the scale inclined in favor of Lincoln as the compromise candidate, and on the third ballot he received the nomination. In the ensuing November election the Presidency was the subject of contention among four candidates, and a total vote of 4,676,853 was cast, divided as follows:

Lincoln, Republican 1,866,352
Douglas, Union Democrat 1,375,157
Bell, Knownothing candidate 587,830
J. C. Breckinridge, pro-slavery Democrat 847,514

4,676,853[10]

If we accept Schurz's figures, according to

[9] *Ibid.*, 68.
[10] McKee, *National Conventions and Platforms*, 118.

which the Germans in 1856 cast 300,000 votes in Illinois, Indiana, Iowa, Michigan, Wisconsin and Ohio, the important share of the German element in the election of Lincoln is pretty conclusively established. But the German vote for Lincoln was much larger. In the States named the total vote from 1856 to 1860 increased 440,223. In the period between 1850 and 1859 immigrants to the number of 976,678 had arrived at American ports, the majority of whom had settled in those States. In Indiana, Michigan and Wisconsin they were given the franchise after one year's residence, and the greater part of the immigrants of the time were Germans. A fair estimate of the German vote for Lincoln in 1860 therefore would be nearer 450,000 than the figure named by Schurz.[11]

The following table shows the relative votes polled by the supporters of Lincoln and Douglas in the States named:

	Electoral Vote[12]	Lincoln	Douglas
Illinois	11	172,161	160,215
Indiana	13	139,033	115,509
Iowa	4	70,409	55,111
Michigan	6	88,480	65,057
Minnesota	4	22,069	11,920
Ohio	23	231,610	187,232
Wisconsin	5	86,110	65,021

[11] Schneider, op. cit., 68, 69.
[12] McKee, op. cit., 118, 119.

If the sixty-three electoral votes of those States had gone to one of the opposition candidates, he would have had 138 votes in the electoral college and Lincoln 114.

CHAPTER IX

The Civil War—Number of Germans in the
Union Army — Their Interest in the Cause —
Fifty-two German-born Generals — Successes
and Failures—Germans Save Missouri—Schurz
and Lieber—German Union Men in the South.

THE United States Sanitary Commission published its "Investigations in the Statistics of American Soldiers," by B. A. Gould, in 1869. The report shows that one-fifth of the volunteers in the Union army were foreign-born. It also shows that 17 per cent of the Germans resident within the United States, according to the census of 1860, were in the army. Gould's table of enlistments[1] gives the following figures:

British-Americans 53,532
English 45,508
Germans 187,858
Irish 144,221
Other foreigners 48,410
Foreigners not otherwise designated 26,445

[1] Quoted in Rosengarten, *German Soldier in the Wars of the United States*, 196.

Rosengarten states[2] that it was not until the war had been waged for sometime that the place of birth was systematically required on the enlistment rolls; the actual records are therefore imperfect. It was not until the organization of the provost-marshal-general's office that nativity was made an essential part of the history of each soldier. Of the 2,500,000 men in the army, the nativity of 1,200,000 was collected for Dr. Gould's work from the records of the national and State capitals, of about 293,000 from regimental officers; and altogether the nativity of 2,018,200 soldiers of a total of two millions and a half was established.

As the result of long-continued investigations and more detailed information, Kaufmann places the number of German soldiers in the Union army at 216,000 men, and inclusive of the first generation, at 500,000,[3] which accords with the estimate of Professor Burgess.[4] Their quota, proportioned to the population, should have numbered not exceeding 128,102, if we accept Gould's figures. The disproportionate character of the quota is

[2] *Ibid.*, Page 194.
[3] *Die Deutschen im Amerikanischen Bürgerkriege*, 118.
[4] *European War of 1914*, 121. He relates that "Mrs. Jefferson Davis, the wife of the Confederate President, has often said to me that without the Germans the North could never have overcome the armies of the Confederacy; and unless that had been accomplished then, this Continent would have been, since then, the theater of continuous war instead of the home of peace."

made apparent from Gould's figures by States, of which only the larger are important here:

	No. of German Soldiers	Proportion to Whole Population
New York	36,680	22,591
Pennsylvania	17,208	13,173
Ohio	20,102	18,984
Illinois	18,140	16,647
Wisconsin	15,709	12,729
Missouri	30,899	7,105

Fundamentally the ardor with which the Germans embraced the cause of the Union was not based upon partisan national feelings, nor, originally, upon enthusiastic sympathy for the negroes, but rather upon an inherent antipathy to that particularism that had been the curse of their own country, and that now threatened to create a cleavage in the country of their adoption, with all the attendant political ills they had but recently escaped. Only in its broader construction did slavery outrage their ideals of human liberty. They had had no share in the making of the slavery laws and they accepted slavery as an established institution. But, as von Holst points out, in the Kansas-Nebraska bill a new law was to be enacted and they would share in its moral responsibilities. For the first time, they were to take a stand on the question. The country was theirs and their children's. "They understood the terrible seriousness of the matter and entered firmly into the struggle as men of independent will and independent thought. They felt themselves Americans and not citizens of this or that individual State. . . . . The arguments for State sovereignty made no impression on them." They inquired merely, "Is the repeal of the Missouri Compromise in the interest of the Union? All the talk as to whether the Missouri Compromise was a 'compact', and as to who made it, seemed to them idle: the fact that it had been looked upon for more than a generation as an inviolable settlement, stamped the Kansas-Nebraska bill in their eyes as an outrageous breach of faith against which German consciousness of right and German rectitude rebelled. . . . Considering their tendency towards political doctrinairism, squatter sovereignty would, perhaps, have had a certain charm for them if it had not been invented solely for the purpose of admitting slavery by a backdoor." To the American the question was complicated—to the German (without the historical background), the question was politically and morally so simple that it could not be recognized as a question at all. "But the Kansas-Nebraska bill devised to extend negro slavery proved wonderfully effective for the political emancipation of the German Americans. They everywhere began to act independently and to withdraw from the camp in which it was wished to make southern principles an absolute party obligation for northern men."[5]

At no time in their history had the German element better qualified leaders—men not only of ideals but of action and daring; men that were not only theorists, but capable, willing and fitted by education and experience to translate their theories into practice. Some of these leaders had sat in the Frankfort parliament and had served on the battle fields in the cause of democracy. The whole system of Southern slave ownership represented a form of landed aristocracy and intrenched privilege that bore an odious resemblance to the European caste system and the widest conceivable diversity from their radical conception of human liberty.

They were among the first to respond to Lincoln's call for volunteers. Carl Schurz put into his traveling bag the pistols he had used in liberating Kinkel, and hastened to Washington. Among the first troops to rally for the defense of the national capital were Germans, notably the Washington and Cincinnati Turners. At the call

[5] *United States*, IV, 426-29.

of Judge Stallo they organized a regiment in Cincinnati within twenty-four hours, and the first contingents in the field as early as the latter part of May, 1861, were the all-German regiments of New York, the 7th, 8th, 20th, 29th and 41st, as well as the 39th, one-half of which was German.

Many of them found suitable assignments in the army. They had served in Europe and now proved efficient instructors in a great number of "mixed" contingents. Their efficiency was especially felt in that arm in which the Northern forces were superior to the Southern from the beginning —artillery. A number became prominent in the engineering corps. Many of the war maps were the work of Germans. The roster of generals and other high officers, according to Kaufmann, contains the names of more Germans than those of any other non-English element. Not a few of these were men of social rank and title, including a von Steuben, Count Zeppelin (as an observer), von Sedlitz, von Wedel, von Schwerin and Prince zu Salm-Salm, whose wife rendered notable service as a nurse.

But those who won high rank did so largely under the handicap and in spite of nativistic prejudice and intrigue, as circumstantially instanced by Schurz in that part of his Reminiscences that deals with the Battle of Chancellorsville. It militated against Sigel after the second Battle of Bull Run, when his participation in important major battles was temporarily suspended and he was assigned to command observation and reserve corps for the protection of Washington and for similar purposes.   While one major-general after another was tried out for supreme command for the Army of the Potomac—Burnside, Hooker, and Meade, after McClellan and Pope — Sigel despite his seniority was ignored.

Kaufmann gives the biographies of 500 German Union officers who won distinction; of these 96 were killed in action, taking no account of those that died of wounds and disease contracted in the service, of whom four were division commanders and brigadiers: Schimmelfenning, Krzyzanowski, Blenker and Asboth.   Fifty-two Germans rose to the rank of General.[6]   The four years of conflict brought into prominence such officers as Sigel, Osterhaus, Schurz, Willich, Stahel, Kautz, Weitzel, Buschbeck, Dilger, Hassendeubel, Wangelin, Weber, Blenker and Bohlen, exclusive of those born in the United States of German ancestry, as Heintzelman, Rosecranz and Custer.[7]

---

[6] Seibel, *Hyphen in American History.*
[7] In the Confederate army the highest rank by a German-born officer was attained by Heros von Borcke, chief of staff to General J. E. B. Stuart, the noted Southern cavalry leader. Von Borcke was a Prussian cavalry officer and inherently a junker aristocrat.

Of approximately 216,000 German-born Union soldiers recruited from a population of some 1,600,000 souls, about 36,000 served in all-German regiments or batteries under their own officers. Of the remaining 180,000 serving in "mixed" regiments, a considerable contingent within the grand army constituted exclusively German companies and battalions.

The first signal achievement, the most important share of the Germans in the entire war, was the holding of the city of St. Louis and the retention of the State of Missouri in the Union. The brilliant achievements in Missouri in the early days of the war were almost entirely overlooked by contemporary historians of the Civil War. Had St. Louis been captured by the Secessionists at that time, the history of the war might have borne a different aspect. It would have been a colossal task to recapture St. Louis—one of the most problematic that could have confronted the Union armies. Instead of the siege of Vicksburg, the siege of St. Louis would have become necessary.[8]

The majority of the people of Missouri were rabid Secessionists and sympathizers with the institution of slavery. Governor Claiborne F. Jackson, a Southern man, feeling assured of the sup-

[8] Young, *Around the World with Grant*, II, 465.

port of an overwhelming Secession sentiment throughout the State, resolved to turn Missouri over to the Confederacy. The first step in this plan was to be the capture of the large Federal arsenal at St. Louis and the subjugation of the city itself. With this end in view he assembled the State troops in St. Louis for inspection and drill at Camp Jackson.

The small garrison at the arsenal was commanded by Captain Nathaniel Lyon, of the regular army, who was a loyal Union man. He quickly perceived the drift of Jackson's plan and determined to anticipate the governor by a prompt counter-move. The question was where to rally enough Union men in a Secession hot-bed that was only waiting for the signal to rise. He was fortunate in finding a kindred spirit in Francis P. Blair, Jr., a Republican politician who had a large acquaintance with the citizens of St. Louis. The loyalists at this time consisted almost exclusively of Germans, a few anti-slavery men of New England origin and the personal followers of Blair.[*]

The gravity of the situation may be inferred from Governor Jackson's reply to Lincoln's call for volunteers: "Your requisition, in my judgment, is illegal, unconstitutional and revolutionary in its objects, inhuman and diabolical, and cannot

---

[*] Snead, *Fight for Missouri*, 57.

be complied with. Not one man will the State of Missouri furnish to carry on such an unholy crusade." Simultaneously the governor sent an autograph letter to the President of the Confederate States requesting him to furnish officers, siege guns and mortars for carrying out his intended attack on the arsenal, and summoned a special session of the Legislature "for the more perfect organization and equipment of the militia and to raise the money and provide such other means as may be required to place the State in a proper attitude for defence."

Blair vouched to Lyon for the loyalty of the Germans and the two quickly agreed upon a plan of action. Blair's activities centered around Turner Hall, which over night became the rallying point of an enthusiastic group of German volunteers. Four regiments were formed, commanded by Blair, Heinrich Boernstein, Franz Sigel and Col. Schüttner. Of these 800 assembled during the night at the arsenal, and on the morning of May 10, 1861, marched out to capture the rebel camp. By 10 o'clock the camp was surrounded and Lyon summoned it to surrender. It was that or fight, and seeing no prospect for successful resistance and no avenue of escape, Camp Jackson capitulated and the prisoners were marched to the arsenal amid howls of derision and rage from the crowds that lined the streets, which vented themselves almost wholly upon the heads of the German loyalists. Riots broke out along the line of march and the Germans were assailed with missiles and cries of "dirty Dutch." The prisoners' procession had hardly got under way when a shot was fired from ambush, and Captain Constantin Blandowski, master-at-arms of the St. Louis Turn Verein, fell to the ground, mortally wounded. His death followed a few days later; he was the first officer to die for the Union.[10]

Lyon's object had been accomplished. The arsenal was saved and St. Louis remained loyal. The power of the Confederacy had been broken at the very beginning; soon, as the troops under Lyon and Sigel spread through the State, Governor Jackson was flying for his life, the Legislature dispersed and Missouri was saved.

Many other brilliant deeds of loyalty and devotion have been obscured, minimized and forgotten in the magnitude of the great panorama of the war; but among the imperishable acts of the four years of slaughter in which a half million lives were lost may be recalled one of the first complete victories of the Union army at Pea Ridge, Arkansas, by Sigel's batteries; the performance of Blenker's division in covering the retreat of the

[10] Kaufmann, *op. cit.*, 201*n*.

Union army after the first battle of Bull Run, July 21, 1861;[11] Willich's *sang froid* in the Battle of Shiloh, and the terrible march of the Germans across the mountains of Virginia.

The German contingents practically everywhere suffered heavy casualties. Of the New York State troops, for example, only 200 survived of the 2,800 men that originally composed the 52d Regiment; of the 1,046 men composing the De Kalb Regiment, only 180 lived to be mustered out; of the surviving 600 men of the 8th Regiment, 220 were killed at Cross Keys. Similarly heavy losses were sustained by the 7th, 20th and 46th, the greater part of them in the desperate fighting in the Peninsular campaign, at Antietam and at Fredericksburg. Of the 103d Regiment only three companies were fit to fight at Appomattox.

Even a hasty survey of the active share of the Germans in the battles of the Civil War would lead to greater length than is here contemplated. In practically all the major battles and in many of the important minor engagements they had a material part. We find Sigel in the West and

[11] Edmund Clarence Stedman in his report of the rout in the *New York World,* wrote: "Only one field officer, so far as my observation extended, seemed to have remembered his duty. Lieutenant-Colonel Speidel, a foreigner attached to a Connecticut regiment, strove against the current for a league." Halsey, *Great Epochs in American History,* VIII, 77.

Blenker in the East making history; we find their countrymen strongly represented at Fort Donelson and Shiloh, the first great battle of the Rebellion; at Corinth, Perryville and under Sheridan at Stone River; executing the march of death through the Virginia mountains in April, 1862, with a loss of 2,000 men in three weeks, arriving at Perryville and Winchester without clothes, tents, shoes, ambulances, provisions, fodder, and practically without ammunition; they were in Pope's campaign in Virginia, sharing the disaster of the second Battle of Bull Run in which Sigel covered the retreat, and in the glory of the Union victory at Antietam as well as feeling the sting of defeat in the terrible reverse at Fredericksburg in 1862, where the Steuben Regiment of New York (the 7th) suffered casualties of a total of 229 men, including nearly half its officers.

They were unjustly held responsible for the loss of the Battle of Chancellorsville, where 125,000 Union troops were defeated by 60,000 Confederates;[12] yet probably the most inspiring single feature of the battle was the heroic defensive action of Buschbeck and Schurz by the former's brigade under his personal command, augmented by part of Schurz's men, which even General Hooker officially complimented. In the face

[12] Cf. Schurz, *Reminiscences*, II, 411-428; Hamlin, *Chancellorsville*, espec. ch. ii.

of 20,000 of Jackson's crack troops, Buschbeck and his 3,500 men retired in one of those
actions that consecrate even a defeat. Taking
Fairview, he notified Hooker of his fitness to
resume the offensive; but the battle was over.

With disaster again came victories, and the
Germans were conspicuous in the triumphs that
crowned the banners of the Union at Gettysburg.
Critical investigators of the war, notably the
Comte de Paris, have accorded General Steinwehr, commander of the second division, full
credit for recognizing the importance of Cemetery
Ridge and obtaining Howard's consent to occupy
this strategic key to the Union position in the
decisive actions of July 2 and 3.[18]

We find the Germans active in Rosecranz's
brilliant but eventually disastrous campaign across
the Cumberland mountains on his march to the
Chickamauga (Chattanooga). Here General
Wagner cleverly maneuvered his 2,800 men so as
to deceive General Bragg into believing he was
dealing with Rosecranz's advance guard, causing
him to evacuate Chattanooga, which Wagner
promptly occupied. The real hero of Chickamauga was General Thomas, who repulsed all
attacks on his position on Horeshoe Ridge, after

[18] Congress gave a vote of thanks to Howard for his prompt seizure
of this important point; Steinwehr was ignored.

the catastrophe, until he could effect an orderly retirement; but Willich's splendid conduct in command of the rear guard is widely acknowledged by military critics, and he and his 32d Indiana German regiment[14] share in much of the glory that attaches to this action as well as to the defense of Horseshoe Ridge, while the German Turner regiment of Cincinnati came in for special praise from Thomas in his official report.

When Longstreet's veterans hurled themselves in a surprise attack on Geary's division at Wauhatchie in the siege of Chattanooga—Geary's men fighting desperately in a dark night and in momentary danger of being pitched into the Tennessee River — it was Schurz and Steinwehr who dispersed Longstreet's forces just in time to avert a disaster; and among the troops that Grant now

---

[14] The 32d Indiana Regiment, drilled and for some time commanded by Willich, earned so many flattering encomiums for its gallantry on many of the most hotly contested battlefields of the war, that the following extract from a reply by Wm. Friedersdorf, a surviving member of the regiment, to an exaggerated account of Terry's Texas Rangers' share in the fight at Rowlett's Station by General John M. Claiborne, deserves a place here, a copy of the letter appearing in Fritsch, *German Settlers and German Settlements in Indiana*, 34, 35. "Instead of 3,000 'federal Dutch' engaged that day, our force did not number over 700, all belonging to the 32nd Indiana infantry. We were called Germans (Dutch by the enemy) but the majority of us were born or raised under the flag which we served—the Stars and Stripes and understood for what we were fighting. We were all American citizens. I think fifty-five of our regiment had seen service in the old country. We received the same pay as other soldiers, and like most of the others, the majority of us could have made much more outside than in the service. . . . If the battle was over 'in a period of four minutes,' that was all the time required by the 'Dutch' to clean up the rangers. They left their dead commander on the field and asked for his remains the next day."

assembled on the battlefields around Chattanooga
we find Schurz, Buschbeck, Steinwehr, Kryzanow-
ski and Hecker of the Army of the Potomac, and
Osterhaus,[15] Wangelin, Willich, Laibold, Conrad
and other commanders of the Army of the West,
hardly a man without a distinguished record.
Osterhaus stormed Lookout Mountain, and a
German officer, Major Hipp, of the 37th Ohio,
won a warm tribute of personal regard from
Sherman when through his expert knowledge of
river navigation and his ingenious employment of
the available means he effected Sherman's safe
crossing of the Tennessee. Here, too—at Missionary Ridge — Buschbeck's brigade again distinguished itself, as testified by Sherman, and here
the irrepressible Willich, in command of nine
regiments, divided the honors with Sheridan in
the storming of Missionary Ridge.[16]

[15] "Leaving one of my best divisions (that of Osterhaus) to act with
General Hooker, . . . I know and feel that it has served the country
well and that it has reflected honor on . . . the Army of the Tennessee."
Sherman's report, War of the Rebellion, Official Records, sec. No. 55,
p. 572.

[16] On Orchard Knob stands Grant. Through his field-glasses he per-
ceives that a major action is in progress, contrary to his orders. He
turns to Thomas. "Did you order that attack?" "Not I," Thomas
replies, adding drily, "That must be old Willich's doings. It looks
like it." Kaufmann, op. cit., 406. Sheridan and Willich's men disputed
the honor of having been the first to reach the top. Among other
German officers who distinguished themselves here were Col. Arnold
Gutermeister's artillery brigade, in which served the German batteries
of Zickerik, Schulz, Fröhlich, Landgräber and Grosskopf; Col. Deimilng,
von Blessing, Kämmerling, Dickermann, Neumann, Cramer, Seidel,
Lochner, Gimber, von Hammerstein, von Baumbach, Beck, Krüger and
Yager, commanding German troops from Ohio, Illinois, Missouri, Pennsylvania, New York and Wisconsin.

The personality of von Willich is so distinctive that his conduct at the Battle of Shiloh to which allusion has been made deserves to be incorporated here in the language of General Lew Wallace describing his share in the battle:

"Facing frontward and looking casually over at our friends of the support, then little more than half-way across their part of the field, I saw they were in grievous straits; that the imaginary cord binding them to their standards had been cut again, and, as before, they were seeking the woods from which they had so newly come out, reminding me of blackbirds in their migratory fall flight.

"I can talk of the circumstances lightly now; but there was nothing light in it then.   And when I beheld the enemy rousing from his concealment, and with triumphant yells preparing to set out in pursuit, I trembled for my division. . . . And now the enemy started forward yelping.   I looked at them, then at the woods behind us in which by that time my supporting force had been lost. Nothing more was to be expected from that force—and, in fact, I saw nothing more of it.   Then—at the last moment, it seemed—from a corner of the field in the south a body not before observed began to file out of the forest.   Who was it?   Friend or foe?

"Shortly the strangers gave me sight of their flag, at which my pulse gave a great jump; for through the glass I could see the stars in the dark blue union with the familiar colors of the morning about them.

"The Confederates swept down until past Woods and his Seventy-sixth, their left flank in easy range.   That was my time, and I should have had the Ohioans on their feet and firing. Few men, however, can always do or say the right thing at the right moment; and I confess to having forgotten everything else, so intent was I watching the up-coming of the strangers.

"They were but a regiment; yet at sight of them the enemy halted, about-faced, and returned to his position in the woods. There he struck out with a fire so lively that the new-comers halted and showed signs of distress. Then an officer rode swiftly round their left flank and stopped when in front of them, his back to the enemy. What he said I could not hear, but from the motions of the men he was putting them through the manual of arms—this notwithstanding some of them were dropping in the ranks. Taken all in all, *that* I think was the most audacious thing that came under my observation during the war. The effect was magical. The colonel returned to his post in the rear, and the regiment steadied as if on parade, advanced in face of the fire pouring upon them and actually entered the wood.

"On my part, then, no time was lost pressing the division forward; and while the order was in delivery I dispatched an orderly to the colonel of the unknown regiment with my compliments and asked his name. 'August Willich of the Thirty-second Indiana Volunteers,' was the reply brought me."[17]

General Sherman reported that Willich's 32d regiment twice repeated the performance on the same day.

The main battle for Kentucky that gave the

[17] *Autobiography*, II, 560-62.

State almost entirely into the hands of the Union forces, that of Mill Springs, January 19, 1862, was decided by the exceptionally furious charge of the 9th (German) Ohio regiment, supported by the 2d Minnesota, one-third of which was composed of Germans.   The entire eastern section of Kentucky and beyond the border of Tennessee, passed under the control of the Union army as the result of that battle.

The fame of the Germans was dimmed by Sigel's defeat at New Market, Virginia, May 15, 1864; but in view of Grant's action in reducing Sigel's army from a force of nominally 32,000 men to 7,000, to solve a problem that eventually enlisted the efforts of 50,000 troops under Sheridan, Sigel's failure presents strong extenuating circumstances and he seems to have been charged with an impossible task.

The fall of Richmond was made possible by Sherman's March to the Sea, the destruction of Hood's Confederate army at Nashville and Sheridan's victories in the Shenandoah Valley.   In Sherman's army on its march south were Osterhaus, succeeding Logan in command of the 15th corps, the heroic Wangelin and his German brigade (3d, 12th, 17th Missouri and the 44th Illinois), the indomitable Buschbeck, Dilger and his famous battery, Brigadier Generals Conrad and Laibold, and

Colonel Winkler with his 26th Regiment from Milwaukee. Kaufmann estimates that Sherman's army consisted of forces one-third of which was German-born or of immediate German descent, but their original formations had by this time been dissolved and merged with the whole and could no longer be identified as distinct units.

The end of the great conflict was at hand. Sherman reached Savannah December 10, 1864, and on Christmas day telegraphed Lincoln that Savannah was taken, and early in January turned north again. Charleston, the cradle of Secession fell; in March Sherman and Schofield joined forces at Goldenboro, N. C., and soon Sherman was at Raleigh, dangerously close to Richmond. Lee might yet have escaped, but starvation stared him in the face and combined against him with his enemies. His veterans had been without rations for several days. On April 9 they capitulated to Grant and famine at Appomattox Court House—25,500 men and 2,802 officers. On April 17 Johnston surrendered to Sherman. A little later the last remnant of this wonder-inspiring army, having fought to the last cartridge, surrendered farther South to Osterhaus. The first to enter Richmond was General Weitzel.

The share of the Germans in the great episodes of the war does not comprise an unbroken chain of untarnished glory; it would not be difficult to name a number of battles which contradict any such inference. But neither would it be difficult to show that their failures were more than compensated by their successes, successes due to their willingness to sacrifice life and property for the preservation of the Union, their failures due no less to circumstances over which they had no control than to unfitness for their allotted tasks. Many a deserving German officer may have had just cause for grievance at finding himself the victim of discrimination and ignored in the bestowal of credit where credit was due, as has been charged; and we are all the more ready to believe that the treatment accorded them in the division of responsibility for disaster was not always impartial when we recall that more than a quarter of a century elapsed before the truth about the Battle of Chancellorsville lifted the blame from the shoulders of the Germans and placed it where it belongs.

· · · · · ·

There were other fields than that of the army in which Germans were serving the cause of the Union. The deserts of Thomas Nast will be referred to elsewhere, as also those of Carl Schurz; but so diversified was the genius of the latter that he was effective both on the battlefield and on the platform at times when conditions demanded the power of his persuasive oratory to keep the war going. Such a time came during the campaign for Lincoln's re-election. In 1864 criticism of Lincoln's administration was loud, and the cry arose, "The war is a failure." It was at this juncture that Schurz leaped into the arena. "The speeches of Winthrop and Seymour," writes Rhodes, "however logical in appearance and finished in expression, were answered in the common mind by the bulletins of Sherman and Sheridan, the decline in gold and in the necessaries of life, and the advance in price and continued large purchases of our bonds in Germany. But persons given to reflection, who liked to see argument met by argument, found matters to their satisfaction in the campaign speeches of Carl Schurz, which, though not seeming purposed as a direct answer to Winthrop and Seymour, shook their positions, demonstrating clearly and cogently the necessity for the re-election of Lincoln."[18]

A man whose services were of a kind not often within the reach and range of a single life, was Francis Lieber. At the outbreak of the Civil War he was quietly settled at Columbia College, New

[18] *United States,* IV, 534-35.

York. As a school boy he served under Blücher at the Battle of Ligny, two days before Waterloo, and was wounded. He came to the United States in 1826 and edited the first American encyclopedia, the *Americana,* in Philadelphia, and after working out an elaborate plan for the management of Girard College, engaged in independent authorship. He was called to the University of South Carolina as professor of history and political economy (1835), and remained there until 1857, when the Secession movement impelled him to resign. One of his sons entered the Confederate army and was killed, another enlisted with the Illinois troops in the Union army; a third was given a commission in the regular army, while Lieber himself began his work as legal adviser to the government on questions of international law. As such he prepared a code of instruction for the government of the armies of the United States in the field, and thenceforth was in continuous employment in related matters, placing his entire vast store of learning at the disposal of the Federal authorities. According to Dr. Holls, a representative of the United States at the first Hague Conference, the idea of codifying and humanizing the laws of war "originated" with Lieber. The humane code, approved and issued by President Lincoln in 1863 as an official government publi-

cation, was universally drawn upon for the formation of international agreements forbidding the
use of poisons, the killing of wounded, the denial
of quarter, the employment of weapons designed
"to cause superfluous injury," pillage, unwarranted
requisitions in conquered territory, etc.   More
rules and by-laws were added later.

Lieber's influence was of great aid to Lincoln
in Germany in creating that sympathy and understanding for the Union cause that translated themselves into heavy purchases of Union bonds at a
time when the government often encountered difficulties in meeting the colossal expenses of the war,
and in the sending of needed medicines, food and
supplies.[19]

Nor can the Civil War be passed over without
mentioning Barbara Frietchie, immortalized by
John Greenleaf Whittier.   Though using a poet's
license, it is not without significance that he
should have selected this Pennsylvania German
woman as the heroine of one of his most popular
ballads.   Barbara Frietchie's maiden name was
Hauser.   Born at Lancaster, Pa., December 3,

---

[19] In a letter of July 18, 1923, to the author, Under Secretary S. P.
Gilbert, Jr., of the United States Treasury Department writes: "Although
it is impossible to ascertain just how many of these (Union) bonds may
have been held in Prussia, according to the report of the Treasurer of
the United States for the fiscal year ended June 30, 1871, 'Germany
had, therefore, next to our own country, been our principal reliance for
disposing of our stocks (bonds)'."

1766, her life thus spanned two great national crises, the Revolution and the War of the States.

. . . . . .

A little-known chapter of the war that deserves attention is that which deals with the tragic experiences of the loyal Germans in the South. The eleven Confederate States contained about 72,000 Germans, scattered over eight States. Only from Tennessee and Arkansas was the road open for German Union men to escape to the northern States. The remaining 52,000 resided in Texas, Louisiana and Virginia. They were overwhelmingly for the Union. Their isolation rendered them practically defenseless. Virginia in 1860 contained 1,047,299 whites, of whom only a few thousand were of German birth; but Virginia contained more people of German descent than any other Confederate State. They were chiefly settled in the Shenandoah Valley and unquestionably formed a majority of the population; however mixed with other blood, they comprised the core of the historic brigade with which Stonewall Jackson's fame is imperishably identified.

Missouri furnished 31,000 German soldiers to the Union army, so that every second man in the Missouri regiments was of that stock. The hatred of the Missouri Confederates for the Germans was inconceivably bitter. German farmers were ruthlessly shot down from ambush, their fields laid waste and their homes burned, because the St. Louis Germans had formed the chief element in crushing the Secession movement by the capture of Camp Jackson. Sigel alone brought more than 1,000 German fugitives to St. Louis from the southern part of the State, and bushwhacking did not cease even after the State had been swept over by the Union armies and nominally cleared of rebels.

In Texas the Germans were called upon to suffer for their loyalty as few others. They fought with unbending tenacity for the faith that was in them against terrible odds, for they were separated by thousands of miles from those who sympathized with them, surrounded by relentless enemies and helplessly exposed to savage cruelties. As regards the Germans, Texas occupied a distinct place among the southern States. A large part of the immigration that poured into the country between 1840 and 1860 settled in that State.[20] In the latter year one-fifth of the white population was German in the first generation and 22,000 were German-born. These colonists were principally concentrated in the southwestern section and out-

[20] Cf. Eickhoff, *In der neuen Heimath.*

numbered the combined English, Irish, French and Spanish population. It consisted of the better educated classes, including many of the "Forty-eighters", and perhaps nowhere else was German life so strongly self-centered and tinctured with uniformly high ideals. Slavery was regarded as an execrable institution. Many of the men were abolitionists of the type of Garrison and Wendell Phillips. The *Deutsche Zeitung* of San Antonio was so violent in its abolition tirades that the Austin *State Times* advised its readers to drown the editor, a threat that would probably have been carried out had not the Germans of San Antonio formed a body guard for his protection.

A typical Texas German settlement was Sisterdale, occupying an ideal locality fifty miles northwest of San Antonio and described as "a little Paradise." The population was of the higher class of refined and educated Germans; almost every house contained a library of scientific and literary books, and the people regularly met for scientific discussion and the cultivation of classic music. This was true of Sisterdale shortly before the war.

What had become of Sisterdale in the fall of 1862? The plantations lay in a state of desolation; the houses were gutted; one prominent man had been murdered by Indians, some of the men were confined in a disgustingly filthy jail in San Antonio, for months, in momentary danger of being lynched. The young men of Sisterdale had almost all been assassinated in the name of the law; their bones were bleaching in the forests of the Neuces, and many that composed the population were hunted fugitives in the mountains, while those who had been confined in jail when finally released, were in constant danger of being shot down by desperadoes. The cause of this unspeakable crime was the fidelity of these Germans and their progeny to the cause of the Union.[21]

Texas seceded February 5, 1861, by a vote of 29,415 to 13,841. The majority of the negative votes was cast by the Germans. Immediately afterwards the storm broke. General Twiggs surrendered the Federal troops under his command to a Confederate mob, together with the San Antonio arsenal, only stipulating that his men might be left free to go north. He himself joined the Confederates with most of his officers. This deprived the frontier of Federal protection and threw it open to the raids of the Indians, riding down from the mountains of New Mexico and Arizona. The troops had no sooner withdrawn .than the Comanches burst in upon the border

---

[21] Kaufmann, *op. cit.*, 143–162. On the settlements before the Civil War see Olmstead, *Journey through Texas*, ch. iii.

settlements, and as most of the outlying farms and plantations belonged to Germans, these received the blow. Barbarously the tomahawk and scalping knife wrought among them. Where possible the borderers fled to the towns, especially to Friedrichsburg, Kerrville and Boerne, the westernmost German communities; but months elapsed before the Confederate militia was able to take the place of the Federal troops, and even then the protection proved inadequate, and the Germans that had been driven from their farms were unable to return to them.

The Comanche raid was only a foretaste of the sufferings still to befall the German settlements. In the words of one writer, "After the red fiends came the white, more savage even than the first, for they ravaged under the color of the law." The Confederate Congress ordered the confiscation of all property belonging to, and the expulsion of, all sympathizers with the Union, those that refused to swear allegiance to the Confederacy and those that had moved out of Texas, leaving their property behind.

Above a thousand Texas Germans had entered the Union army in Missouri or by way of Monterey and Matamoras, whence they were sent north by sea. They had left their families and their property behind, and while the latter fell into the hands of the enemy, the former were abandoned to indescribable misery. This was followed by legislation under which men who had spent their lives in Texas were stripped of everything they possessed in the turn of a hand.[22] This law fell heaviest upon the German settlers along the western border of the State. After the proclamation of martial law, the home of every Union sympathizer was outlawed. Those that had escaped to the north might consider themselves fortunate, for those that tried to escape later were persecuted with remorseless savagery; they were pursued and most of them killed.

"To convert Union men to the true faith by means of the halter" became literally true. Referring to the German Unionists, the San Antonio *Herald*, according to Lossing, wrote: "Their bones are bleaching on the soil of every county from Red River to the Rio Grande, and in the counties of Wise and Denton their bodies are suspended by scores from the 'Black Jacks'."[23] The raids were inaugurated by a Vigilance Committee with headquarters at San Antonio; its president was a well-to-do business man and a shining light of the Methodist Church. The ostensible purpose of the secret organization, which adminis-

---

[22] H. H. Bancroft, *Texas*, II, 458.
[23] *Pictorial History of the Civil War*, II, 536.

tered punishment only with the halter, was the suppression of the desperadoes with which Texas was infested; but the Vigilantes consisted wholly of Secessionists, members of the Knights of the Golden Circle. The *Records of the Rebellion*[24] contain documents relating to the widespread persecution of German Union men, many of whom had remained on their farms in the hope that the war would soon be over. A requisition on General Magruder for troops to assist in the compulsory impressment of German Union sympathizers was answered with orders to expel from the State all strangers who refused to enlist in the Confederate army, but advised caution. A report that 1,500 Germans were concealed in the mountains near Friedrichsburg afforded an excuse for sending troops into the German part of Texas to relieve the Vigilantes and nominally to restore order. The only foundation for this report was that about 500 young men of German parentage had called a secret meeting at Bear Creek and had taken an oath to resist enlistment in the Confederate army. A party of 65 men belonging to this group resolved to escape to the north under Fritz Tegner. They were surprised at the Neuces and more than half their number were killed.

A Confederate detachment under one Dunn,

[24] Cf. Sec. No. 21, pp. 886-87.

acting as provost-marshal, issued a proclamation granting three days within which all Union sympathizers—described as "bushwhackers"—were ordered to come into camp or be treated as traitors. The time was far too short to reach those whom it concerned, even had it been honestly intended as a period of grace. A searching party sent out returned with ten Germans from the neighborhood of Friedrichsburg. Under the pretext that they had essayed to escape, the ten patriots were summarily hanged to the limbs of trees.

A general hunt for German Union men now began, and lasted the whole summer. Dunn sent parties out that brought back not a single prisoner; only one party returned with four or five men, eight women and many children. The men were thrown into jail (and afterwards lynched); the women and children found shelter in Friedrichsburg. R. H. Williams reports that in ranging about the Neuces River he inspected the scenes where his comrades had raged and ravaged. Everything had been destroyed, the fields as well as the houses; the furniture had been broken, the cattle and horses driven off; the inhabitants had disappeared.[25]

During the four years of war hundreds of Ger-

25 *With the Border Ruffians*, 235-38.

man settlers, many of whom had fought the Indians side by side with their tormentors, were murdered in cold blood.²⁶ But neither exile nor violence was able to break the love of these men for the Union, and though their families were forced to pay the penalty and those that remained were constantly exposed to assassination; though, even as late as April, 1865, ten German patriots were dragged from the jail at Friedrichsburg and hanged to trees in the outskirts of the town, they resisted conscription to the end of the war. The official war records speak of the protests of these Germans in the so-called Beigel settlements and of battles with the Germans in Medina county in 1863 and even in 1864.

   [26] Olmstead says that the Texas Germans formed more than fifty per cent. of the Rangers who in the '50s fought with the Federal troops against the Indians. *Texas,* 302.

CHAPTER X

Intellectual Contributions in Literature, Art,
Science and Education—Captains of Industry—
Astor and Sutter — Carl Follen's Influence —
William Wirt and Gustave Memminger—Generals
Armistead, Quitman, Custer — Molly
Pitcher.

WE have so far followed the Germans — possibly
rather episodically—in their relations to the
newly-formed State and society on the North
American continent as pioneers, pathfinders,
cultivators and soldiers. The history of the German
element is largely typified in the careers of
individuals. Their influence never appears in the
form of mass control, and only at times in the
form of mass direction, as in Pennsylvania preceding
and during the Revolution, and again in the
election of Lincoln in 1860 and the ensuing
period of the war for the preservation of the
Union. On the other hand, hardly any other
national or racial stock performed more valuable
"team work", or, in the form of outstanding individuals
of capacity, gave more of intellectual

value, or set higher examples of constructive patriotism in the work of rearing the political edifice, than the German element. We find nowhere in their history proof of a desire to take a detached political attitude, but rather striking uniformity of purpose to sink their individuality in the great aggregate, like disciplined members of a conquering army.

Whether in art, science or business, the student is confronted with names of men whose deeds cannot be lightly disregarded; even a cursory inspection of the annals of the German race in America reveals how important is the contribution to the commonwealth of ideas for which we are indebted to German immigration. "The Germans are not merely our brothers; they are largely ourselves. The debt we owe to German blood is great; the debt we owe to German thought and to German example . . . . is even greater."[1]

The first large American chemical works were started by Germans in Philadelphia. The father of homeopathy in the United States was Dr. Konstantin Hering. Few, if any, scientific men have shed greater luster on America than Samuel David Gross, the famous surgeon, whose *Elements of Pathological Anatomy* (1839) attracted the favorable notice of Virchow, and whose *System of*

---

[1] Roosevelt, *New York Times*, October, 1914.

Surgery (1859) marked a great advance in surgical knowledge and practice. He was of valued service during the Civil War, largely in the work of providing artificial limbs. His brilliant achievements were widely recognized and rewarded with such honors as the presidency of the American Medical Association (1862), of the International Medical Congress, at Philadelphia in 1876, the D. C. L by the University of Oxford at its 1000th anniversary, and the LL. D by the Universities of Cambridge, Edinburgh, Pennsylvania, and Jefferson College. The highest honors were accorded Dr. Gross' memory when in 1897 a heroic statue of him—to which Congress contributed the granite pedestal—was unveiled in Washington, D. C. Dr. Gross was born in Pennsylvania and was a descendant of the Palatines. His father was a well-to-do farmer who was connected with the quartermaster's department during the Revolution.

Another distinguished Pennsylvanian of German descent was Dr. Joseph Leidy, born in Philadelphia in 1823, a descendant of the Germans who hailed from the Rhinelands. Dr. Leidy was noted for his investigations of the extinct fauna of America and published the *Special Anatomy of the Terrestrial Mollusks of the United States* as well as a number of monographs on the extinct fauna of South Carolina, Dakota, Nebraska and the West.[1a]

The founder of the great banking house of Drexel & Sons, on which the international banking firm of Morgan & Co. is in turn founded, was Franz Martin Drexel, born in 1792 in Dornbirn, Tyrol. He left home to escape the Napoleonic invasion, and, after painting portraits in Milan for a living, came to the United States in 1817. Joseph Seligman, born in Bavaria in 1819, who established another great banking house, played a prominent diplomatic role during the Civil War, and is in some quarters credited with floating a considerable amount of Union bonds, estimated by the late Senator Stewart of Nevada at approximately $500,000,000, in Germany in 1862. The

[1a] Under date of December 6, 1923, the Associated Press sent out a dispatch from Philadelphia announcing that "Many national and international scientific societies will participate in the centenary celebration of the birth of Joseph Leidy, hailed as one of the greatest zoologists of the last century, to be held in the Academy of Natural Sciences.

"One of the features of the observance will be the establishment of a memorial medal in honor of the scientist. It will be known as the Joseph Leidy medal and will be awarded from time to time in recognition of preeminent contributions of biological science. It will be placed as a trust with the Academy of Natural Sciences.

"Dr. Leidy, born here September 9, 1823, was connected with the Academy of Natural Sciences from 1845 until his death, April 30, 1891. He is called the greatest of American scientists, 'The American Cuvier,' and 'the father of the study of fossil vertebrate animals in America.' His achievements covered every branch of natural history. During his life he wrote 553 papers and articles on plants, minerals and biological subjects. For forty-eight years he served as professor of anatomy at the University of Pennsylvania, from which institution he was graduated in 1844."

establishment of the first building and loan association is credited to Dr. Wilhelm Schmole of Philadelphia; Joseph Ripkow started the textile industry in Monajunk, Penn., and the famous Steinway piano works were established in 1850 by Heinrich Engelhard Steinweg, born in Brunswick in 1797. William Havemeyer brought with him from Germany in 1799 a knowledge of the business of refining sugar, and his industry became the foundation of the modern sugar business. The vast iron and steel works of Pennsylvania are almost exclusively of German origin, long antedating the activities of other men of German descent who were still, or were until recently, identified with this industry, as Schwab and Frick. Likewise the famous yacht builders, the Hereshoffs, trace their origin to a German immigrant, as does John Wanamaker, former Postmaster General and one of the pioneers in the department store business. John D. Rockefeller is a descendant of one of the Palatines sent by Queen Anne to Ireland, who arrived in the United States early in the eighteenth century. The builder of the Northern Pacific Railroad was Henry Villard, born in Bavaria, who arrived in the United States at the age of eighteen without resources and without a knowledge of the English language, and overcoming one difficulty after another, became a well-known war correspondent during the Civil War *(New York Herald* and Greeley's *New York Tribune)* and finally a railroad magnate. He married a daughter of William Lloyd Garrison, the abolition leader.

Among the noted German men of affairs in America John Jacob Astor stands out as pre-eminent. He was born in Walldorf near Heidelberg, July 17, 1763, the son of a butcher, who succeeded in driving all his sons from home by the violence of his temper. An elder brother was engaged in the fur trade in New York, and young Astor came to America in 1783 after spending several years in London with another brother. He took service with a kind-hearted Quaker tanner in New York City, who recognized his worth and sent him out into the wilderness of upper New York State as a buyer of pelts and hides. In 1786 Astor engaged independently in the fur trade, and in 1809 founded the American Fur Company in opposition to the Hudson's Bay Company, establishing the pioneer American trading post on the Pacific, the fur supply station Astoria. Here for the first time on the Western coast was hoisted the American flag over a permanent settlement, but the enterprise practically came to grief as a result of the war of 1812. Astor founded the Astor Library in New York at an outlay of $400,000 and gave a site on Lafayette Place. When the government found itself in a desperate state of financial stringency to conduct the war (1812-14), he proved his faith by investing heavily in its securities. Among the first American ships in the oriental trade were those sent out by Astor (1800), who was determined to break the English monopoly of this important carrying trade and loaded his vessels with furs, ginseng, iron and lead for China and brought back teas and other commodities supplied by the Orient.[2] He was president of the German Society of New York, from 1841 to 1845, which he liberally supported with his means, and on his death left $50,000 to his native village for a school for poor children and a home for the aged. Astor was the friend of Washington Irving, Fitzgreen Halleck and other noted literary men of his time, in whose work he expressed a sincere interest.[3]

[2] "At that time no American vessel traded at Canton. The East India ports were as tightly closed to American commerce as if they had not existed. . . . John Jacob Astor was America's pioneer merchant in the China trade. Following in his wake were a hundred other merchants, who made large fortunes in the years that followed." Gebhard, *John Jacob Astor*, 132, 135.

[3] "It is not because of the success of this intrepid promoter that the founding of Astoria occupies such a unique position among the great exploits in the history of American expansion. His attempt to secure the fur trade was not a success; but, considering the day in which it was conceived, the tremendous difficulties to overcome, the rivalry of British and Russian promoters in the North and Northwest, and the inability of others to achieve it, the founding of Astoria on the Columbia must be considered typically American in the optimism of its conception and the daring of its accomplishment. If there is a good sense in which the

Against the historic background of the settlement of the Pacific Coast stands out in luminous outlines the figure of John August Sutter. John Jacob Astor had attempted, unsuccessfully, to found an American colony on the western coast. He had been the first to hoist the flag over an American settlement in that remote and inhospitable section of the continent. Sutter is said to have raised it for the second time as an emblem of permanent sovereignty. Born in Kandern, Grand Duchy of Baden, Sutter received an excellent education; graduated from the military school at Thun, and, after serving in the Swiss army and acquiring Swiss citizenship, he came to America in 1834. At St. Louis, then the outfitting point for the Santa Fe trail and center of the fur trade, he joined an expedition to Santa Fe and returned with substantial profits. His next trip was undertaken with an American fur trading expedition. Crossing the Rocky Mountains he reached Fort Vancouver, headquarters of the Hudson's Bay Fur Company, in September, 1838. In 1839 he arrived in Monterey and decided to carry out a long-cherished plan of founding a colony on the

words can be used, America has been made by a race of gamblers the like of which the world has never before seen. We have risked our money as no race risked money before our day. Astor was perhaps the first great 'plunger' of America; his enthusiasm carried everything before it and influenced the spread of American rights and interests." Hurlbert, *Pilots of the Republic*, 289.

Sacramento River. On a strip of land 120 miles northeast of San Franciso, which he acquired from the Mexican governor, Alvarado, he founded the settlement of New Helvetia and built Fort Sutter. He then offered inducements to settlers and broke several hundred acres of land, on which he built a tannery, a mill and a distillery. About 1840 his livestock consisted of 20,000 head of cattle, horses and sheep. Many settlers established themselves around his fort, and, having secured title to his lands from the governor, he was appointed the official representative of the Mexican government for Northern California. In 1844 he laid out the town of Sutterville on the Sacramento River, which latterly took the name of Sacramento. In 1848 he planted the first vineyards . north of Sinoma. His wheat crops were estimated at above 40,000 bushels annually for various years, while his large commercial and industrial enterprises promised him a steady increase of his fortune, even then estimated at millions.

Encouraged by Major Frémont, the Pathfinder, who visited Fort Sutter in the Spring of 1846, Sutter on July 11 declared his independence of Mexico and with the appearance of Commodore Stockton's squadron and the American invasion of

Mexico, California became a territory of the United States.[4]

A tragic turn in the fortunes of this typical pioneer set in when, in January, 1848, in digging the foundations for a new mill on the American River, a tributary of the Sacramento, J. W. Marshall, one of Sutter's employes, discovered gold. Despite Sutter's efforts to keep the discovery a secret until he had completed his mill and settled his land titles, the news leaked out and circulated with the speed of a prairie fire. Thousands of gold-hunters poured in, over-ran his lands and staked claims, while farming and cultivation were paralyzed by demands for fabulous wages, as every able-bodied man turned prospector. Countless lawsuits had to be instituted in the attempt to dislodge thousands of adventurers who had squatted on Sutter's lands, and titles became worthless. The courts decided against him in one of the Mexican grants, and other misfortunes coming apace, Sutter found himself reduced to poverty. In allowances for taxes paid by him the

[4] "In the cycle of the coming years historians will write of the founding and settling of this western State, and when they shall dwell upon the virtues, the hardships, the sufferings and courage, the valor which has brought all this about; when they describe the mighty impulse which this commonwealth has exercised upon the progress of free government and the development of the principles of liberty, and when they shall adorn the annals with the names of the founders of its fame, no name will illuminate their records with a more brilliant light than that of the immortal Sutter — the noble example of the California pioneer." Edward J. Kewen at the banquet of the Society of California Pioneers, September 9, 1854.

State granted him an annuity of $3,000 for seven years.   In 1865 Sutter turned his back upon California, a ruined man, and died at Litiz, Pennsylvania.

Sutter's great service was not recognized until later years.   He was broad-minded, generous and hospitable, with a strong adjunct of courage, shrewdness and the intellect for great conceptions. His name was given to rivers, towns and counties, and the room of the legislative hall was adorned with his portrait.   During his prosperous days he had been elected a major-general of the State militia and in 1849 he was a member of the constitutional convention.   No story of our pioneering days can surpass the pathos of Sutter's rise and fall.   Speaking of the discovery of gold on Sutter's farm, Mowry[5] writes: "It was this simple discovery that changed entirely the political history of our country," and General Sherman: "To General John A. Sutter more than to any other man our country is indebted for California and all its wealth."[6]

The first white man to explore the mountain wilderness of the Pacific side of the continent was the Jesuit Father Eusibio Francisco Kino (Eusibius Franz Kühn), who reached America

[5] *Territorial Growth of the United States,* 101.
[6] Koerner, *Das Deutsche Element,* 298.

either in 1680 or 1681. Before the conquest of Canada by the English and during the days that witnessed the arrival of the Pilgrims of Germantown and the Leisler regime in New York, this heroic German priest, toward the latter part of the eighteenth century penetrated Arizona as far as the Gila River at its junction with the Colorado. In 1731 Philip V ordered three missions to be established in Arizona at the royal expense, and three German Jesuits, Fathers Keller, Grasshoffer and Segesser, were sent. About 1750 Father Sedelmayr, at the instance of the Spanish government, was evangelizing the tribes on the Gila, erecting seven or eight churches in the villages of the Papagos.

A famous contemporary of Astor in the South was William Wirt, prosecutor of Aaron Burr and a distinguished orator, Attorney General of the United States under three administrations, first appointed by Monroe. His father was a native of Switzerland and his mother of Wurtemberg. He was born at Bladensburg, Md., and was left an orphan at an early age. Having been admitted to the bar in 1792 he opened an office at Culpeper Court House, Va. He was a young man of agreeable qualities and great vivacity, and after a short, aimless career, settled down to a sober life of study "preparing him to meet such opponents as Thomas

Jefferson, James Monroe, Daniel Webster." He
went to Richmond in 1799, and there met all the
great men of the State and occupied various offices.
As counsel to prosecute Burr, he delivered the
speech that is one of the most admired of oratori-
cal efforts and was long a favorite for academic
declamation. Judge Story ranked him "among
the ablest and most eloquent of the bar of the
Supreme Court." He received the degree of
LL. D. from Harvard in 1824. In 1832 he was
the anti-Masonic candidate for President, and
received seven electoral votes. Even better known
than his addresses and essays were his *Letters of
a British Spy* and his *Life of Patrick Henry*. He
moved to Baltimore in 1829 and died in 1834.
Wirt never forgot his German antecedence and in
1833 engaged in founding a colony of Germans in
Florida, but the venture was not successful.

A German, born in Wurtemberg in 1803,
Gustave Memminger, occupies a prominent place
in the history of the South. After serving nearly
twenty years in the South Carolina legislature,
mainly as chairman of the committee on finance,
he was elected State Treasurer in 1860 and at the
outbreak of the Civil War was appointed Secretary of the Treasury in the Confederate Cabinet
under Jefferson Davis. This position he held until June, 1864. He then resumed his law practice

and became president of the Charleston & Ohio Railroad Company. Down to the outbreak of actual hostilities, he was strongly in favor of the Union.

Some notable engineering feats owed their inspiration and execution to Germans, who, as in many other expert branches, came over richly equipped by careful training for their professions, thus giving their adopted country the benefit of their knowledge and experience without putting it to the cost and trouble of providing the necessary education. A considerable number of expert engineers of German birth were active in the Civil War, and a prominent example in private life was John August Roebling, born in Mühlhaussen, June 12, 1806. He graduated at the Berlin Royal Polytechnic School in 1826 and came to the United States in 1829, settling in Pittsburgh, where he began the manufacture of iron and steel cables, which he discovered could be efficaciously used in the building of bridges. In the bridge over the Alleghany River at Pittsburgh, whose construction he directed, the first suspension wire cables ever seen in the United States were used; and in 1851-55 he constructed, what was regarded as one of the wonders of the world, the suspension bridge across the Niagara River. Roebling worthily closed his career in 1869 with his plans—approved by eminent engineers—for the Brooklyn Bridge across the East River, New York City, completed by his son, Washington Augustus, who was born in Pennsylvania in 1837.

One of the most successful bridge builders in the United States, still living, is Gustav Lindenthal, constructor of the Hell Gate bridge at New York, said to be one of the most perfect works of the kind in the United States, and among the foremost of electrical engineers and inventors was Charles P. Steinmetz, the associate for many years of Edison. The ancestry of Westinghouse, whose fame has spread to all parts of the world, too, harks back to a German immigrant, according to an authorized biography of the great inventor.

Among the leading American architects of German antecedence the names of Johannes Smithmeyer and Paul J. Pelz are prominent as the architects of the Congressional Library in Washington, and among the noted sculptors we must name Albert Jaegers, the creator of the Steuben statue in Lafayette Park, Washington, executed by order of Congress, and of the Pastorius historic monument at Germantown, Penn. A number of well-known names may readily be added: Karl Bitter, Joseph Sibbel, Charles Niehaus, Albert Weinman, F. W. Ruckstul, Otto Schweitzer and Professor

Bruno Schmitz, the designer of the Indianapolis monument. The first teacher of Hiram Powers, whose Greek Slave is still one of the most cherished treasures of American art, was Friedrich Eckstein of Cincinnati.

In literature, as historians, essayists, poets and novelists, the Germans and their descendants take a far more prominent part than is generally supposed. The first American dramatist who may be credited with the distinction of genius, as already indicated, was Godfrey, the son of the inventor of the quadrant, who died before his talents could be fittingly acknowledged. An intellectual woman of distinguished literary ability and German birth was the wife of Professor Robinson, *nee* von Jacob, who wrote under the nom de plume of Talvj. Her works include *Ossian Not Genuine*, (Dublin, 1841), *Heloise, or the Unrevealed Secret, The Exiles, Woodhill,* and other studies and novels. She was a friend of Washington Irving and other noted Americans of her day. Hermann Ernst Ludwig was the author of *Literature of American Local History* and *Literature of American Aboriginal Languages;* Herman Kriege wrote a German work, *Fathers of the Republic,* published in a series of pamphlets with the object of presenting the heroes of the Revolution to his countrymen as political models; Isaac Nordheimer was the author of a Hebrew grammar, *History of Florence, Hebrew and Chaldee Concordance* (with Professor Turner); Dr. George I. Adler composed a German grammar, a *German-English Dictionary* and wrote a *Manual of German Literature;* and Karl Goepp created an international sensation by the publication of his pamphlet, *E Pluribus Unum,* in which he exploited the idea of the United States becoming the agent of universal governmental regeneration and the rallying point of all nations; he also translated Auerbach's village stories into English, and was the successful candidate of a non-partisan movement for judge of the New York Marine Court. Friedrich List wrote *Outlines of a New System of Political Economy,* one of the earliest expositions of the theory of the protective tariff; and among those of the same stock who contributed their learning to the subject of political economy were Francis J. Grund, author of a great variety of works in English on topics ranging from politics to astronomy, and Dr. Johann L. Tellkampf, prominent in educational and prison reform movements and a member of the commission to revise the laws of the State of New York.

The first place among German writers who made their home in the United States belongs to Dr. H. von Holst, author of the monumental work, *Constitutional and Political History of the United States*, and we may here refer to Carl Schurz as a spiritual brother of Holst. Carl Schurz's career not only influenced American political life—he was one of the leaders of the civil service reform movement, which he put into practical operation while Secretary of the Interior under President Hayes—but he shone as a patriotic orator and writer. His *Henry Clay* is widely credited with being the best biography in the American Statesmen's series, and his autobiography, *Reminiscences of Carl Schurz*, is a work of great value and literary refinement. Schurz was the first native German that ever occupied a place in the cabinet.

Historical writers are Friedrich Kapp, Anton Eickhoff, Wilhelm Kaufmann, Oswald Seidensticker, Professor Julius Goebel, Rudolph Cronau, Otto Lohr, H. A. Rattermann, Gustav Koerner, and numerous others, whose works deal with the Germans in the United States. Of these the exhaustive work of Professor Faust,[7] of Cornell University, *German Element in the United States*, published in two volumes in English, is the most complete and satisfactory. No writer to-day can

[7] Albert Bernhard Faust, born in Baltimore, Md., in 1870, author of a number of historical and literary works and of valuable monographs on American history.

deal with this subject without going to Faust to consult his exhaustive source of information. Kapp wrote the lives of General von Steuben and DeKalb, a history of the Germans in the State of New York, a work on slavery in the United States, on the traffic in soldiers of certain German princes, etc. He was New York's commissioner of immigration and later became a member of the German Reichstag. Anton Eichkoff wrote an interesting work on the German element. He was appointed by Governor Seymour of New York on the commission to provide for the comfort of the New York troops after the Battle of Gettysburg, was Secretary of the Democratic executive committee, a member of the State Legislature, coroner of New York City, and a Representative in Congress from the Seventh New York district. Seidensticker was the author of historical works that particularly dealt with early German life in Pennsylvania.

We have in another place spoken of a group of German novelists of distinction; we will here refer briefly to a little coterie of poets and essayists who stand out among a number of brilliant native writers: Herman George Scheffauer, George Seibel, Herman Hagedorn, Henry L. Mencken, Rudolph Lewissohn, George Sylvester Viereck, and Theodore Dreiser. Among the German-language poets mention must be made of at least two of surpassing interest: Konrad Kretz and Konrad Nies. A poem by Kretz, dedicated to his fatherland, written during the Civil War, is marked by the highest poetic touch and is instinct with tenderness and feeling. Bret Harte had a German strain in his blood; Dr. Fritsch informs us that the Hoosier Poet, James Whitcomb Riley, was of German extraction; but no native American author was so completely mastered by German thought and influence as Bayard Taylor, whose two grandmothers were German. Joaquin Miller had German forebears; and among the descendants of the original Palatine settlers of Pennsylvania are several poets, historians and essayists of eminence and marked originality, at least one of whom won fame by his verse written in the Pennsylvania-German dialect. One of America's greatest actors, Edwin Forrest, had a German mother, as had Maude Powell, famous violinist, to whom she attributed her love of music.

A survey of the academic field within which the Germans were conspicuous throws into relief the name of Carl Follen of Harvard, whose influence was so far-reaching in association with George Ticknor, A. P. Peabody, Emerson, Margaret Fuller, Longfellow and the Transcendentalists in making popular the study of German literature and the German language,[8] and who was so largely instrumental in introducing German athletics into American colleges.   At Harvard University he lectured on moral philosophy and ethics.   A master of English, he was likewise a brilliant orator. In the list of educational pioneers an honored place belongs to Mrs. Carl Schurz (nee Margaretha Meyer), who opened the first kindergarten in the United States, at Watertown, Wisconsin, in 1855.

One of the most learned theologians, who wrote a number of works in the English language, was Philip Schaff; Isaac Leeser was another prolific author on theological subjects; Prince Gallatzin was the founder (1798) of the Catholic Mission of Loretto in Pennsylvania; Johann N. Naumann, Catholic bishop of Philadelphia, was the author of religious and botanical works, *Ferns of the Alleghanies* and *Rhododendrons of the Pennsylvania and Virginia Mountains*.

Save Remington, none has painted more graphic pictures of the American frontier than Charles

---

[8] It is at least significant that the enthusiasm for the study of German and German literature and philosophy during this period is coincident with the golden age of American literature, the generation of Ticknor, Edward Everett, George Bancroft, Longfellow, Motley, G. H. Calvert, B. L. Gildersleeve, Francis J. Child, E. T. Harris, G. M. Lane, W. D. Whitney, Th. D. Woolsy, George L. Prentiss, George William Curtis, Timothy Dwight, H. B. Smith, F. H. Hedge, W. C. King and B. A. Gould, all of whom studied at German universities. Cf. Goebel, *Journal of English and Germanic Philology* for January, 1923.

Schreyvogel, notably in his painting, "My Bunkie", and among the foremost American painters whose names survive are Emanuel Leutze, the painter of "Washington Crossing the Delaware" and "Westward the Star of Empire", the latter in the capitol at Washington, and Albert Bierstadt, the painter of the Yosemite Valley, whose great works adorn the Senate side of the national capitol and many of the art galleries of Europe. Other noted American painters of German birth or antecedence are Carl Marr, Carl Wimar, Toby Rosenthal, Henry Twachtman, F. Dielman, Robert Blum, Gari Melchers, Henry Mosler and A. Nahl of California. The front rank of American cartoonists is occupied by two German-born artists, Thomas Nast and Joseph Keppler, the founder of *Puck*. Nast, the creator of the elephant and ass as the emblems of the Republican and Democratic parties, respectively, exerted a tremendous social and political influence during his career, chiefly as cartoonist for *Harper's Weekly*. "Very early in the war he led his public to a realization of the necessity of abolition, and with his ardent and fearless pencil he stiffened the Northern mind. 'Thomas Nast has been our best recruiting sergeant', said Abraham Lincoln near the close of the Civil War; 'his emblematic cartoons have never failed to arouse enthusiasm and patriotism, and have always seemed to come just when these articles were getting scarce'."[9] General Grant attributed more influence in winning the war to Nast than to any other individual in private life.

Who will say that American musical history would not have had an entirely different character had it not been for the many able German musicians who about the middle of the nineteenth century established themselves in a great number in all of the larger as well as smaller communities throughout the country as the directors of singing societies, creators and conductors of great orchestras and as teachers of singing and musical instruments? We can but gratefully remember the pioneer work of Theodore Thomas in carrying the cult of classic music into the remotest corners of the land and thus establishing standards of taste that quickened American life with a new ideality.

· · · · · ·

Before closing we may presume to add to the roster the names of three famous soldiers whose deserts will never be forgotten as long as the republic shall glory in the memory of patriotic deeds. The commander of Fort McHenry in the

---

[9] Faust, *op. cit.*, II, 361.

war of 1812, Major George Armistead, was of direct German descent, his ancestors, having come from Hesse-Darmstadt and settled in the Shenandoah Valley, at New Market, Va., where he was born on April 10, 1780. He entered the army as second lieutenant in 1799. In 1813 he had the rank of major in the Third Artillery and was distinguished at the capture of Fort George. His gallant defense of Fort McHenry in 1814 won for him immortal renown; for his heroic defense he was given military advancement and his action has been commemorated with a monument in Baltimore. It was his heroic defense of Fort Mc-Henry that was the immediate cause of the writing of "The Star-Spangled Banner."

Another descendant of the Hessians who helped to make history at a later day was General George A. Custer, famous cavalry leader and martyr of the Little Big Horn Indian massacre of June 25, 1876. The name was originally Küster.

General John Anthony Quitman, one of the heroes of the Mexican war, was the son of Rev. Friedrich Heinrich Quitmann, a native of Rhenish Prussia, a highly gifted man and learned author, who was active not only in religious matters but in political life as well, being elected to the legislature of New York State and holding the position of president of the Lutheran Ministers'

Association of New York from 1807 to 1828. His son, the future general of the American army, was born at Rhinebeck, N. Y., September 1, 1798. He became professor of German at Mount Airy College, Pennsylvania, and then studied law and began practice at Chillicothe, Ohio. In 1827 he removed to Natchez, Miss., received the appointment of chancellor of the Supreme Court of the State and was elected a member of the legislature and presiding officer of the latter. He participated in the liberation of Texas, and visited France and Germany, being appointed a member of the Supreme Court of Mississippi soon after his return. At the outbreak of the Mexican war he enlisted as a volunteer, was appointed brigadier general in 1847 and promoted to Major General by President Polk. For his bravery at the battle of Monterey he received a sword from Congress and he had his full share in the daring deeds by which General Scott's troops forced their entrance into the Mexican capital. On September 13, 1847, at the head of his brigade, he stormed the supposedly impregnable heights of Chapultepec under the very muzzles of the Mexican guns. Returning to Natchez after the war he was elected governor of Mississippi and from 1855 to the time of his death represented the Natchez district in Congress. He was an ardent seccessionist but died before the Civil War.

We may here insert a brief notice commemorating a heroine of the Revolution, Molly Pitcher, whose racial origin has given rise to some dispute. Her maiden name was Maria Ludwig, and she was born in Pennsylvania in 1744, of Palatine ancestry. In 1822 the Pennsylvania legislature granted her a special pension for life. She died in the following year and was buried with military honors. On her monument at Carlisle, Pa., her name appears as Mollie McCauley (renowned in history as Molly Pitcher, the Heroine of Monmouth), the latter being the name of her second husband. A monument on the battlefield of Monmouth represents her in the act of ramming a cannon. She also appears in G. W. Parke Custis's painting, "The Field of Monmouth."[10]

. . . . . .

A general survey of the animated picture of German activities and achievements reveals the great influence of the German element in the Making of America: Their sufferings and heroic endurance as pioneers among the outposts in the American wilderness, down to 1862-1863 in Minnesota and in Texas; their devotion to liberty,

[10] Faust, *op. cit.*, 341, II, 463*n*.

as attested by their uttering the first protest
against slavery; Leisler's leadership of the first
popular party and his convoking of the first colonial congress; Zenger's successful fight for the
liberty of the press; their share in reversing the
attitude of Pennsylvania from opposition to one
that aligned Penn's province with its sister colonies in favor of independence; Conrad Weiser's
statesmanlike service in tranquillizing the powerful Indian tribes when peaceful development was
so vital to New York, Pennsylvania and Virginia;
Christian Frederick Post's mediation in breaking
the French-Indian alliance; Zeisberger's earliest
settlement of the region now composing the State
of Ohio; their early invasion of the dark and
bloody ground of Kentucky and their settlements
there.   We discover their momentous share in
settling not only Pennsylvania, but Virginia,
Georgia and the Carolinas; their great number of
experienced and intrepid woodsmen, hunters and
pathfinders, and their influence in changing the
wilderness into rich farms and plantations and
their early development of infant industries.
Their descendants may well point with pride to
the heroic battle of Oriskany, fought by the Mohawk Palatines under Herkimer, because of its
effect on the defeat of Burgoyne at Saratoga,
which Creasy calls the decisive battle of the

Revolution;[11] the valuable service of General Steuben as the real organizer of Washington's patriot army. Later we trace the steady influence of the Germans on American life in the promotion of scientific and skilled practices in the industries, resulting in the phenomenal expansion of trade and manufacturing, their prominence in science and education; we witness Astor's epochal transcontinental expedition, his development of the American fur trade, his share in breaking up the English monopoly of the carrying trade with the Orient and the winning of that traffic for American bottoms. They help manfully in the winning of the West. Among the pioneers in Texas are Germans. They are among the earliest in California. Far out on the Pacific coast the American flag is hoisted by a German-born American. On his land the first gold is found. We find them represented in all our wars and domestic crises; they make possible the election of Abraham Lincoln, hold Missouri in the Union under Lyon and Blair, steady the loyal sentiment in Maryland and help to hold Kentucky. They lay the foundation of the great iron and steel industry; in the forefront among the giants of the electrical field

---

[11] "Creasy does not mention here the battle of Oriskany, which, combined with the unsuccessful siege of Fort Stanwix, obliged St. Leger and his Indians under Joseph Brant to return to Oswego." Halsey, *Great Epochs in American History*, III, 158n.

stands Charles P. Steinmetz; the mechanics of printing are revolutionized by Ottmar Mergenthaler, inventor of the linotype.

Thus, as settlers, pioneers, explorers, soldiers, inventors and merchants they have played their part alongside the pioneer races in the building of the republic.

Bibliography

BABCOCK, KENDRIC CHARLES, *The Rise of American Nationality, 1811-1819.*

BAER, GEORGE F., *Germans in Pennsylvania.*

BANCROFT, GEORGE, *History of the United States*—Final ed.

BANCROFT, H. H., *N. Am. States and Texas.*

BECKER, CARL L., *The Beginning of the American People.*

BENTON, NATHANIEL S., *A History of Herkimer County including the Upper Mohawk Valley.* Albany. 1856.

BERNHARD, DUKE OF WEIMAR, *Travels.*

BITTINGER, LUCY FORNEY, *The Germans in Colonial Times. German Religious Life in Colonial Times.*

BOSSE, GEORG VON, *Das deutsche Element in den Vereinigten Staaten.* 1908.

BURGESS, JOHN W., *The European War of 1914. The Civil War and the Constitution.*

COBB, SANFORD H., *The Story of the Palatines.*

CAMPBELL, DOUGLAS, *The Puritan in Holland, England and America.*

CRONAU, RUDOLF, *German Achievements in America.*

DEILER, J. HANNO, *The Settlement of the German Coast of Louisiana and the Creoles of German Descent.*

Deutsch-Amerikanische Geschichtsblaetter.

DIFFENDERFER, FRANK RIED, *The German Immigration into Pennsylvania Through the Port of Philadelphia, 1700-1775.*

DOYLE, JOSEPH B., *Frederick William von Steuben and the American Revolution.* 1913.

EASTBURN, IOLA KAY, *Whittier's Relation to German Life and Thought.*

EICKHOFF, ANTON, *In der Neuen Heimath; geschichtliche Mitteilungen über die deutschen Einwanderer in allen Teilen der Union.*

ELSON, HENRY WILLIAM, *History of the United States.* 1 Vol. 1904.

FAUST, ALBERT BERNHARDT, *The German Element in the United States.*

FISHER, SYDNEY GEORGE, *The Making of Pennsylvania.*

FISKE, JOHN, *The American Revolution. The Dutch and Quaker Colonies in America. Old Virginia and Her Neighbors.*

FORCE, *Am. Archives.*

FORD, HENRY JAMES, *The Rise and Growth of American Politics.*

FORSYTH, MARY ISABELLA, *The Beginning of New York; Old Kingston the First State Capital.*

FRANKLIN, BENJAMIN, *Writings.* (Smith, ed.)

FRITSCH, WILLIAM A., *German Settlers and German Settlements in Indiana.* Evansville, 1915.

GEBHARD, ELIZABETH L., *The Life and Ventures of the Original John Jacob Astor.* 1915.

GOEBEL, JULIUS, *Das Deutschtum in den Vereinigten Staaten von Nord-Amerika. Der Kampf um das Deutschtum, 16.* München, 1904.

GREEN, J. R., *A Short History of the English People.*

GREENE, EVARTS B., *Provincial America.*

GRIFFIS, WILLIAM ELLIOT, *The Influence of the Netherlands in the Making of the English Commonwealth and the American Republic.* A Paper Read Before the Boston Congregational Club, October 26, 1891. *The Romance of American Colonization.* Boston, 1898.

HALSEY, FRANCIS W., ed., *Great Epochs in American History Described by Famous Writers. The Old New York Frontier.*

HAMLIN, AUGUSTUS C., *The Battle of Chancellorsville.* Bangor, 1896.

HARPER'S *Encyclopedia of American History.*

HART, ALBERT BUSHNELL, *American History Told by Contemporaries.*

HASSALL, ARTHUR, *The Balance of Power, 1715-1789.* 1907.

HEITMAN, FRANCIS B., *Register and Dictionary of the U. S. Army.*

HERRIOTT, F. I., *Germans of Chicago and Stephen A. Douglas in 1854,* in Deutsch-Amerikanische Geschichtsblaetter, XII. Chicago, 1912.

HENDERSON, ERNEST F., *A Short History of Germany.*

HEYER, W. C., *Anna Weiser Mühlenberg.*

HOFMANN, JULIUS, *A History of Zion Church of the City of Baltimore, 1755-1897. The Germans of Maryland During the Colonial Period.*

HOLST, H. VON, *Constitutional and Political History of the United States.*

HURLBERT, ARCHER BUTLER, *Pilots of the Republic.*

JENKINS, CHARLES F., *The Guide Book to Historic Germantown.* Germantown, 1908.

KAPP, FRIEDRICH, *Die Deutschen im Staate New York waehrend des achtzehnten Jahrhunderts.* With an introduction by Carl Schurz, 1884. *Life of General von Steuben.* Introduction by George Bancroft.

KAUFMANN, WILHELM, *Die Deutschen im Amerikanischen Bürgerkriege.* München, 1911.

KOERNER, GUSTAV, *Das Deutsche Element in den Vereinigten Staaten von Nordamerika, 1818-1848.* Cincinnati, 1880.

KNAUSS, JAMES OWEN, JR., *Social Conditions among the Pennsylvania Germans in the Eighteenth Century as Revealed in the German Newspapers Published in America.* 1922.

KUHNS, OSCAR, *The German and Swiss Settlements of Colonial Pennsylvania. A Study of the So-Called Pennsylvania Dutch.* 1900.

LAMB, MARTHA J., *History of New York.*

LECKEY's *History of the Revolution.*

LEE, RICHARD HENRY. *Life of Arthur Lee.* 1829.

LESTER, C. EDWARDS, *History of the United States.*

LINCOLN, C. H., *The Revolutionary Movement in Pennsylvania.*

LODGE, HENRY CABOT, *A Short History of the English Colonies in America.* 1904. *The Story of the Revolution.* 1903.

LOHR, OTTO, *The First Germans in North America and the German Element of New Netherland.* 1912.

LOSSING, BENSON J., *Eminent Americans. Pictorial History of the Civil War.*

MACAULAY, *Works.*

McKEE, *National Conventions.*

MACDONALD, WILLIAM, *Select Documents of United States History.*

McMINN, EDWIN, *A German Hero of the Colonial Times of Pennsylvania; or, The Life and Times of Henry Anthes.* 1886.

MARSHALL, JOHN, *Life of Washington.*

MYERS, L. C. V., *Life and Adventures of Lewis Wetzel.*

Minute Book of the Committee of Safety of Tryon County, N. Y. 1905.

MORRIS, CHARLES, ed., *Half Hours with American History.*

MOWRY, WILLIAM A., *The Territorial Growth of the United States.*

OLMSTEAD, F. W., *A Journey Through Texas.* N. Y. 1857.

PARKMAN, FRANCIS, *Montcalm and Wolfe. The Conspiracy of Pontiac.*

PASTORIUS, *Circumstantial Geographical Description of Pennsylvania.* Frankfort and Leipsig, 1700.

Pennsylvania Colonial Records.

PENNYPACKER, SAMUEL WHITAKER, *The Settlement of Germantown, Pa., and the Beginning of German Emigration to North America.*

PFISTER, ALBERT, *Die Amerikanische Revolution.*

REEVES, *Wineland the Good.*

RHODES, JAMES FORD, *History of the United States.*

RICHARDS, GEORGE W., *The German Pioneers in Pennsylvania.*

RICHARDS, H. M. M., *The German Leaven in the Pennsylvania Loaf.* Wilkes-Barre, 1907.

ROOSEVELT, THEODORE, *The Winning of the West.*

ROSENGARTEN, J. G., *The German Soldier in the Wars of the United States.* 2d ed., Phila., 1890.

RUTHERFORD, LIVINGSTON, *John Peter Zenger: his Press, his Trial, and a Bibliography of Zenger Imprints.* N. Y., 1904.

SACHSE, JULIUS F., *The True Heroes of Provincial Pennsylvania.*

SCHNEIDER, OTTO C., *Abraham Lincoln und das Deutsch-*

thum, in Deutsch-Amerikanische Geschichtsblaetter, VII. Chicago, 1907.

SCHRADER, FREDERICK F., *Prussia and the United States; Frederick the Great's Influence on the American Revolution.*

SCHURZ, CARL, *The Reminiscences of.*

SCISCO, LOUIS DOW, *Political Nativism in New York State.*

SEIBEL, GEORGE, *The Hyphen in American History.*

SEIDENSTICKER, OSWALD, *Bilder aus der Pennsylvanischen Geschichte.*

SIMMS, JOSEPH ROOT, *Trappers of New York.*

SMYTH, JOHN F. D., *Tours.*

SNEED, THOMAS F., *The Fight for Missouri.* 1886.

SPARKS, EDWIN ERLE, *The Men Who Made the Nation.*

STILLÉ, *Wayne.*

STONE, *Brant.* (1865).

STOKES, I. N. PHELPS, *The Iconography of Manhattan Island.*

TURNER, FREDERICK JACKSON, *Rise of the New West, 1819-1829.*

Virginia Magazine.

WALTON, JOSEPH S., *Conrad Weiser and the Indian Policy of Colonial Pennsylvania.*

WALLACE, LEW, *An Autobiography.*

War of the Rebellion, Official Records.

WEST, WILLIS MASON, *Source Book in American History and Government.*

WASHINGTON'S *Writings.*

WHEELER'S *Historical Sketches of North Carolina.* 1851.

WHITE, ANDREW DICKSON, *Autobiography.* 2 Vols., N. Y., 1907.

WILLIAMS, R. H., *With the Border Ruffians.* London, 1907.

WILSON, WOODROW, *History of the American People.*

YOUNG, *Around the World with Grant.*

INDEX

Everett, Edward, 249.

Fabian, Rev. Peter, 144.
Fairchild, Henry Pratt, 9.
Faust, Dr., 38, 39, 67, 72, 75,
120, 129, 130, 144, 167, 172,
188, 246, 251, 254.
Fechten, A. V., 125 (Van Vech-
ten).
Fedder, Valkert, (Vedder), 125.
Finck, Andrew Jr., 122, 123.
Fink, Andreas, 124.
Fink, John, 173.
Fink, Michael, 170.
Fischer, 124, 136, 157 (or Viss-
cher or Visgar).
Fiske, 35, 51, 53, 55, 86, 88,
127, 141, 181, 182.
Fonda, Adam, 124.
Fondersmith, Johann, 94.
Forbes, Brig. General, 171.
Follen, Carl, 248.
Forrest, Edwin, 248.
Forsyth, 50.
Fox, Christian W., 124.
Fox, Christopher W., 122, 123.
Fox, Frederick, 124.
Franck, J., 124.
Franklin, Benjamin, 82, 83, 84,
88, 108, 113, 114, 177.
Frederick the Great, 130, 141.
Fremont, John C., 188, 189, 191,
237.
Frelinghuysen, Gen. Frederick, 54.
Frelinghuysen, Rev. Theodore J.,
54.
Frey, Johann, 125, 126.
Frey, John, 122, 123, 124.
Frey, Samuel Ludlow, 121.
Friedeisdorf, William, 210.
Frick, 233.
Frietchie, Barbara, 219 (Hauser).
Fritsch, Dr., 210, 248.
Frohlich, 211.
Fuchs, Christian W., 125.
Fuchs, Friedrich, 126.

Fuchs, William, 66.
Fuller, Margaret, 248.

Gallatzin, Prince, 249.
Gansevoort, Colonel Peter, 135.
Garrison, William Lloyd, 222,
234.
Geary, 25, 210.
Gebhard, 235.
Gerlach, 72, 73.
Gerstaecker, Frederick, 183.
Gestern, Juli, 117.
Gilbert, Secretary S. P. Jr., 219.
Gilderstein, B. L., 249.
Gimber, 211.
Girty, Simon, 147.
Godfrey, 44, 88, 244.
Goebel, 144, 154, 181, 246, 249.
Goepp, Judge, 191.
Goepp, Karl, 245.
Gottfrieds, 44.
Gould, B. A., 196, 197, 198, 249.
Graeff, Abraham Op Den, 42.
Graeff, Dirck Op Den, 42.
Graeff, Herman Op Den, 42.
Graeff, Margaretha Op Den, 42.
Grant, 210, 211, 214, 215.
Grasshoffer, Jesuit Father, 240.
Graydon, Alexander, 108.
Greene, 102, 104, 182.
Griffis, Dr., 39, 54, 145.
Grimm, Francis, 191.
Gross, Samuel David, 230, 231.
Grosskopf, 211.
Grund, Francis J., 245.
Gutermeister, Col. Arnold, 211.
Gwinn, William, 166.

Hacke, Dr. Nicholas, 39.
Hagar, Jonathan, 165.
Hagedorn, Herman, 247.
Hagerhoffs, Maria, 44.
Haggin, John, 172 (Hagen).
Hallmer, Frederick, 124-6 (Hell-
mer or Halmer).

Printed in the United Kingdom by
Lightning Source UK Ltd., Milton Keynes
138111UK00001B/95/A